MW00333097

The
Fawn Brook Inn
Cookbook

The
Fawn Brook Inn
Cookbook

ALLENSPARK, COLORADO

Hermann and Mieke Groicher

JOHNSON BOOKS
BOULDER

Copyright © 2008 by Hermann and Mieke Groicher

All rights reserved.
No part of this publication may be reproduced or transmitted
in any form or by any means, electronic or mechanical, including photocopy,
recording, or any information storage and retrieval system,
without permission in writing from the publisher.

Published by Johnson Books, a Big Earth Publishing company
3005 Center Green Drive, Suite 220, Boulder, Colorado 80301
1-800-258-5830
E-mail: books@bigearthpublishing.com
www.bigearthpublishing.com

Cover and text design by Rebecca Finkel
Cover photo © James Frank, www.jamesfrank.com

9   8   7   6   5   4   3   2   1

Library of Congress Cataloging-in-Publication Data
Groicher, Hermann.
The Fawn Brook cookbook / Hermann and Mieke Groicher
p.   cm.
Includes index.
ISBN 978-1-55566-413-8
1. Cookery. 2. Fawn Brook Inn.
I. Groicher, Mieke. II. Title.
TX714.G7685   2008
641.5—dc22   2008003126

Printed in China by Oceanic Graphic Printing, Inc.

Contents

Stocks, Reductions, Hot Sauces, Cream Sauces, Butter Sauces, Glaces, Syrups, and Flavored Butters

Vinegars, Salad Dressings, Concentrated Herbal and Spiced Oils

Concentrated Herbal and Spiced Oils

Appetizers

Pâtés and Terrines

Soups

Hot Clear Soups

Hot Cream Soups

Garnishes for Hot Soups

Side Dishes

Entrées

Complete Gourmet Dinners

Starting with an aperitif, appetizer, soup, salad, main entrée,
wine selection, dessert, coffee, and after dinner drinks.

x

For our four grandchildren
who are a great blessing from the Lord.
As all four of them love to eat,
it is my hope that they remain true to the old saying:

"Essen und drinken halten leib und seele zusammen,
Bonne Appetite."

(Eating and drinking keep together body and soul)

Adrieke and Nemonie

We moved to the Fawn Brook when I was five years old. One of the families that made regular visits to the natural spring across the street was the Donahue family. They just happened to have a daughter, Nemonie, the same age as me. We became instant friends, more like sisters than anything else.

The stairway that led from the restaurant to our home above is a very narrow and steep one—perfect for sliding. At that time there was no barrier built in the restaurant to separate the stairs from the restaurant. Nemonie and I found it great fun to wait for my mom to pass by so we could say good-night, and by some act of God each time would result in us simultaneously "falling" down the stairs and out onto the dining room floor of this romantic restaurant.

xiv

Panhandling

As I've become a mother, I've realized that I need to shield certain regular customers of the Fawn Brook from talking to my children. Not too long ago I was talking to old friends and they brought up the memory of a very poor child who never got any food from her parents. Ironic that this child lived in a gourmet restaurant. She and her best friend decided the best way to nourish themselves would be to panhandle from the restaurant guests. As you've most likely guessed, this sad child was me and my best friend, the infamous Nemonie. We would move from table to table telling our sad tale of poverty, hoping for scraps to fill our empty bellies. More often than not, after shocked looks from the customers, we would be able to feed ourselves properly for the night.

About Hermann and Mieke Groicher

Hermann Groicher was born in 1936 to Kajetan and Hermine Groicher in the small mountain village of St. Lambrecht, Austria. He shared his daily responsibilities on the family farm with his eleven siblings. His grandparents owned and operated a "Gasthaus" (inn) in the same village of St. Lambrecht. After eighteen years in the small community high in the Austrian Alps, Hermann traveled to Switzerland to start a career in the hotel/restaurant business. After a three-year study, he was advised to start traveling and working in different places to enrich his knowledge and to gain new perspectives. This brought him to different areas around Europe, ending in Cardiff, Wales. After three years in Cardiff, he immigrated to the United States when the Hotel Corporation of America sponsored him to continue his trade in Houston, Texas. During his time in Texas, Hermann had the honor and privilege to prepare table-side a Caesar Salad for some of the first astronauts!

Mieke Groicher was born in 1935 to Hendrik and Adriana Hoogendoorn in the town of Gouda, Holland. Mieke had two older brothers, Cees and Pieter. Hendrik was an accomplished organist and shared his gift with many young people. He was very involved in the community, primarily with the youth, but also helped his father in a family owned cigar factory. Mieke's mother held the family together teaching them strong morals and a love of helping people. Mieke followed in her mother's footsteps and has a profound gift for helping people, which led her to the path of becoming a nurse. Mieke's nursing career brought her from Holland to England and to Wattenwil, Switzerland in 1966. One of her patients was Hermann's Aunt Fanny. Hermann had come to Switzerland to visit with his aunt and met Mieke. There was an instant attraction and three days later they were engaged to be married. Six months later, they were married—almost forty years ago!

Hermann's culinary skills continued to grow and in 1969 he had the opportunity to move to Boulder, Colorado, to work as the head chef at the Greenbriar Restaurant. During that time, Boulder was a "dry" city but through a lot of hard work and perseverance and the assistance of an incredible family friend and confidant, Lou Winterberger, they opened the first bar in the city of Boulder. The Catacombs, in the Boulderado Hotel, was a historic opening and remains in business today.

In October of 1970, they had their first child, a son, Kajetan (Ki-YA-ten). While attending college in Lindsborg, Kansas, Kajetan met his wife Kara. He and Kara have blessed Hermann and Mieke with two grandchildren, a boy and girl, Cayden and

Anneliese. They are currently deployed overseas where Kajetan serves as an Intelligence Officer with the United States military. Kajetan has inherited quite a lot of Hermann's talent in the kitchen, which may explain his acumen as a biochemist.

In November of 1973, Hermann and Mieke had their second child, Adrieke (A-DREE-ka), their daughter. Adrieke and her husband, Chris Osmun, live in Poway, California, where Chris serves in the United States Marine Corps. They also have given the gift of grandchildren, two boys, Alex and Nicholas. Adrieke does not have the culinary flair, but son Alex is determined to become the next Hermann Groicher.

During a family trip to the mountains in 1979, they found the Fawn Brook Inn. At the time it was a family restaurant and just happened to be for sale. With their friends Jim and Lucielle Morehouse, the partners purchased the business and began major renovations. In addition to remodeling the restaurant portion, the upper floor was converted into a home for Hermann, Mieke, and their children. In 1985 Hermann and Mieke bought out their partners and became the sole owners of the restaurant.

Mieke in 1979 on their first visit to Fawn Brook.

Since 1979, the Fawn Brook Inn and the Groicher family have been known not only for Hermann's fine food but for their hospitality. Mieke's presence in the restaurant is equal to that of Hermann's with her grace and genuine character. The restaurant still thrives today with a clientèle that comes from all over the world to enjoy the magical experience of dining at the Fawn Brook Inn. It has become not only a place for far away visitors but for the local residents as well. It hosts an annual Christmas Eve service, charity dinners, community lunches, soup ministry, Fourth of July popsicles, family celebrations, and engagements. It is a destination for annual anniversary and birthday dinners and is a much anticipated occasion for customers and friends. The Fawn Brook is a destination where everyone who visits immediately feels like family.

—ADRIEKE OSMUN (GROICHER)

ACKNOWLEDGMENTS

I HAVE A THANKFUL HEART for my Creator who blessed me with a talent beyond my imagination. Thank you dear God for giving me the wisdom and for always staying on my side as this book was created.

A HEARTFELT THANK YOU needs to go to my beloved wife of forty years, Mieke. Over the many years, as I was working on these recipes, she always extended her patience and compassion, even at times when I did not deserve it. Her fortitude did not waiver. Most of all I thank you, Mieke, for an understanding heart and mind, especially in times of frustration and madness (which occur on occasion).

THANK YOU TO OUR CHILDREN, Kajetan and Adrieke, for the support, advice, and helping hands. I could never have done it alone. A very special thank you to my daughter, Adrieke, for transforming my foreign handwriting into something legible, all the while juggling her busy life with her husband, raising two boys, and a full time job. Thank you again.

THANK YOU TO OUR FRIENDS David and Phebe Novic of the Warming House in Estes Park. Thank you for your prayers, encouragement, and suggestions. A special thanks to David for helping in the process of actually creating edible goods. Thank you for having the courage to sit down with Mieke and myself to eat those creations, as each of us either got fat, lost weight, or sometimes even got sick. I figure there must be something worthwhile in this book!

THANK YOU to David and Robin Knox of Boulder, dear friends of great value, who helped evaluate the recipes and for getting them ready for the publisher's desk. I could have never done it without your help, you are both greatly appreciated.

THANK YOU to the many guests at the Fawn Brook Inn, who over the years gave the encouragement and support needed. Quite a few of you even became great friends.

LAST BUT NOT LEAST, to Mira Perrizo, Linda Doyle, Molly Morgan Hazelrig, and Rebecca Finkel of Johnson Books for their faith, advice, and reassurance; but most of all for taking on the publishing of this book. Thank you from the deepest of my heart.

AND TO ALL OF YOU who are reading and using this book, may it be a blessing to each one of you.

THANK YOU AND GOD BLESS,
Hermann and Mieke

Fawn Brook Inn, circa 1920.

HISTORY OF THE FAWN BROOK INN

Following is a letter written in 1992 by Mabel Downer Durning, which gives an insight to the history and significance of our restaurant. Mabel was one of our first customers and became one of the many favorites we've been fortunate enough to meet over the years.

In the 1920s it was Allen's Park, but in the 1890s–1910s it wasn't even Allen's Park. The village location was the George Pfeiffer homestead. Allen lived five miles east. Allen didn't have anything to do with the village area. Or, according to Vera Rubendall, "Allen was a squatter, not a homesteader. He just turned cattle loose in the mountain area during the balmier part of the year. Took them to the valley warm!" Take your choice!

'Taint easy to tell the story of the Fawn Brook Inn but we have a few clues as well as two or three handed-down stories, some may or may not be true!

Apparently B.K. (unclear of initials) Bailey built not only the Fawn Brook, but Highlands Ranch, Crystal Springs, and a number of rental cabins located behind McAllister's filling station near Fawn Brook in the late 1910s–1920s. The logs, like the ones used by the church, came from the Pole Patch on the Ironclads. These were ideal building material because a forest fire had sealed in the log resin and made them much stronger than the usual cut. They slid the logs down the mountain to the spot where they were loaded on wagons to be moved to the building sites. Most of the historic fire-killed log structures in the village were built with the same materials at about the same time.

Fawn Brook Inn has apparently had seven owners. Bailey (1920s), Ann Wetig (don't know anything about her or when she ran the Inn), Augusta Mengedoht (1930s), John and Rose Reinhold, Dick and Mary Beth Alford, John and Kathy Richards (1960s), and Hermann and Mieke Groicher. There is one owner missing since the Richards said, "We are only the fifth owners."

If the structure was built in the 1910s–1920s era, that meant outdoor privies, no indoor plumbing or electricity. The Bailey family was an early day builder and developer of the area and came with considerably more financial resources than the local homesteaders. They were also Episcopalians, along with a number of others in the area, who helped finance and build St. James on the Mount [now the Community Church of Allenspark]. Their son Ben Bailey, now a well-known artist, painted the triptych that used to grace the church altar, and it has since been removed and placed in the Estes Park museum as part of the Allenspark historical display. The Bailey daughter, Marcita, continues to visit the Allenspark area when she returns to Colorado.

You cannot tell the story of Fawn Brook without telling about Augusta Mengedoht. She alone is worthy of an entire novel, her background is so interesting. As briefly as possibly

Augusta and some of her friends.

by fitting together a few clues, I believe Augusta came to Lyons, Colorado, as a young girl. Possibly she had a tuberculosis scare. She returned to Omaha, Nebraska, where as a daughter of a wealthy family, she was raised in a very protected environment. We have pictures of her playing tennis and swimming. Both she and her sister had extensive musical training—the sister a pianist, Augusta a concert violinist. Augusta was married to an artist who turned out to be extremely violent. Newspaper articles describe the judge in Omaha directing him never to set foot in Omaha again. Following the divorce Augusta received a letter from Walter Ufer, one of the early 1900s Taos artists, known as the "Taos Terror," telling Augusta to start standing on her own two feet, making her own decisions, and stop being sheltered. Those of us who knew Augusta in her later life can hardly believe this to be the same woman who led hunting parties that came and stayed at the Fawn Brook! She went to the Hamm Hardware store in Longmont, ordered (and got!) dynamite to loosen the rock in the Fawn Brook basement, did her own horseshoeing, helped put a tin roof on the Inn with the help of Charley Eagle Plume, possibly did some of the plumbing and electrical work, served on all kinds of Allenspark improvement committees, and still cooked, cleaned, and managed the Fawn Brook Inn! Allenspark has always had their share of characters and Augusta ranks right up there at the top of the list.

Fawn Brook Inn, 1938.

John and Kathy Richards were owner-managers in the 1960s when a number of younger people moved to the mountains hoping to find a new way of life. During their ownership it was the gathering spot for all walks of life, young and old.

Following the Richards, Hermann and Mieke Groicher and their two young children took over. Previous experience at the Greenbriar (at Left Hand Canyon and Foothills Road) gave them a running start with a devoted clientele who appreciated good music, gourmet food, excellent service, European ambience, and a welcoming flower garden—all in a rustic mountain setting, which is now known throughout Colorado. Nothing, however, prepared them for the back-breaking labor of bringing the basement storage, food preparation area, living quarters, and other parts of the Inn up to standard after many years of neglect.

One of my fondest memories of the early-day Groicher ownership was watching their two well-trained children at a table in the dining room playing games or using coloring or cutting books to occupy their time during the days when Fawn Brook served lunch as well as dinner.

The Groicher ownership of Fawn Brook Inn has been a very positive and colorful addition to everything that goes on in the little mountain village, which is nestled at the base of a ring of beautiful mountains: The Ironclads, Meadow Mountain, Wild Basin, Copeland Mountain, Chiefs Head, and a fourteen-footer known as Mount Meeker. A fitting setting for a very lovely Inn such as Fawn Brook.

DINING ROOM "FAWNBROOK INN" ALLENSPARK COLO.

Abbreviation of Measurements

PINCH: a very small amount (approximately 1⁄16 tsp)

DUSTING: a light coating

DOLLUP: a small glob of soft food, or a "splash" of liquid

DASH OF LIQUID: about 1⁄8 tsp

TABLESPOON: Tbsp

TEASPOON: tsp

OUNCE: oz

POUND: lb

1 CUP: 8 oz

2 CUPS: 1 pint: 16 oz

4 CUPS: 2 pints: 1 quart: 32 oz

8 CUPS: 4 pints: 2 quarts: 1⁄2 gallon: 64 oz

16 CUPS: 8 pints: 4 quarts: 1 gallon: 128 oz

One must also keep in mind that liquid forms are always measured in cups. Loose forms such as flour, ground nuts, etc., should always be measured by the ounce on a scale, as they are much lighter, and 1 cup is not necessarily a full 8 oz.

In all recipes, white pepper is used, always freshly ground. The salt I use is either kosher salt or refined coarse sea salt. Kosher salt is pure refined rock salt. It does not contain magnesium carbonate and therefore it will not cloud liquids when added. Sea salt is pure—it has no added substances and is quite a bit stronger and much healthier than regular table salt.

In this book, all cooking, baking, poaching, roasting, etc., is done at high altitude on propane gas and is measured in Fahrenheit degrees. Adjustments are most necessary at lower elevations with natural gas or electric operated equipment.

GLOSSARY OF SOME COMMON KITCHEN TERMS

A LA CARTE: a menu term signifying that each item is priced separately.

AL DENTE: firm to the bite, not over-cooked, such as vegetables and pasta.

AU BLEU: a freshly killed fish; *trout* is plunged into an aromatic boiling court bouillon; it turns the skin a metallic blue color.

AU GRATIN: a crusted top, achieved by high heat, on casseroles sprinkled with cheese, bread-crumbs, or cheese infused cream sauce. Use hot oven or top broiler.

BAKE: foods cooked in an oven surrounded by hot, dry air. A usual term used for breads, pastries, and baked goods.

BÉCHAMEL SAUCE: a basic white sauce consisting of some liquid, cream, aromatics, and thickening agent. Many other sauces are derived from it for fish and fowl.

BEURRE BLANC SAUCE: a classic white sauce consisting of herbal wine reduction, cream, and butter; excellent with fowl, fish, and as a vegetable coating.

BLANCHE: a technique to very quickly parboil any vegetable in mildly seasoned boiling hot water for a very short time, depending on the density of the product.

BOIL: any food item that needs to be boiled in liquid for a certain amount of time.

BOUQUET GARNI: a sachet or tied-up cheese cloth containing herbs and spices used to flavor stocks and sauces.

BRAISE: a method to tenderize certain tough, leafy vegetable greens. Tie desired portion of greens with a non-toxic string. Place them in an oven-proof container, lightly sprinkle with sea salt, add a little water or broth, sprinkle with butter and cover with lid and braise in preheated oven to desired doneness. Shock them right away with ice water to stop cooking process.

TO BRAISE MEAT: (any tough muscled meat: briskets, chicken) Season with salt and pepper and very lightly brown on all sides in a skillet in desired hot fat. Place on a bed of mirepoix in roasting pan, add just a little liquid to it, cover and braise until desired doneness is achieved. *Some meats may need marinating before braising.*

CARAMELIZATION: the browning of sugar over high heat.

CLARIFIED BUTTER: melted butter from which all milk solids and water have been removed. Because solids have been removed and water has evaporated, clarified butter may be used for cooking at higher temperatures.

COMPOUND BUTTER: creamed butter seasoned with herbs, garlic, chives, salt, and so on.

CONCASSÉ: a coarsely chopped mixture of tomatoes, garlic, and onions.

CONSOMMÉ: a richly seasoned flavorful broth, clarified, clear, and transparent.

COURT BOUILLON: water seasoned with herbs, root vegetables, salt, and lemon. Used to poach fish.

CROUTONS: small bread cubes that are seasoned, sprinkled with oil and lightly browned in the oven.

DEEP FRY: foods cooked by submerging in hot oil.

DE-GLAZE: done by heating a small amount of liquid—wine or stock—in the skillet and stirring to loosen browned bits of food from the bottom of the pan. The resulting mixture becomes the base for the sauce accompanying the prepared food.

DEMI-GLACE: a rich brown sauce fortified with Madeira or sherry, reduced and used for many other sauces.

DOUBLE BOILER: a double pan arrangement whereby the two pots are formed to fit together with one sitting partway inside the other. The lower pot holds the simmering water that gently heats the mixture in the upper pot. It is used to warm or cook heat-sensitive foods, such as custards, delicate sauces, and chocolate.

DREDGE: to dip food items in flour, egg wash, and bread crumbs or finely grated cheese before pan frying.

DRESSED: a term used for fowl and fish. The food item has been completely cleaned and can be used as is for cooking.

DUXELLES: a combination of finely chopped mushrooms, shallots, and herbs slowly cooked in butter until it forms a thick paste. It is used to flavor sauces, cream soups, and also the famous goose liver pâté for Beef Wellington by adding chopped truffles to it.

EGG WASH: It has various uses in the kitchen, especially for use on pastry dough. Use two whole eggs and one egg yolk mixed well with 1 Tbsp milk and a pinch of salt and pepper.

EN CROÛTE: a food item usually partially cooked or grilled, then wrapped with or without a filling in a pastry case, egg washed, and baked.

ESCALOPE: term for a very thin, usually flattened, slice of meat or fish.

FINE HERBS: a mixture of finely chopped fresh herbs, the classic quartet is chervil, chives, parsley, and tarragon.

FLAMBÉ: a dramatic method of food presentation. It consists of sprinkling foods with brandy liqueur, which after warming, is ignited just before serving.

FLEURON: small decorative shaped puff pastries baked and used as garnish, mainly for fish and cream soups.

FLUTE: to press a decorative pattern into the raised edge of a pie crust, or to carve slashed grooves and other decorative markings in vegetables, mushrooms, etc., used for garnishing purposes.

FOIE GRAS: the liver of specially raised geese and ducks. A must for classic foods, such as Beef Wellington and Tournedos Rossini. It's very delicate and expensive.

FOOD MILL: an old kitchen utensil, best described as a mechanical sieve. Its hand-turned paddle forces food through a strainer plate removing skins, seeds, and fiber. Most come equipped with several interchangeable plates. A very useful and timesaving tool.

FOOD PROCESSOR: a very modern kitchen appliance. If properly used, it can ease hour-long preparation methods.

FORCE MEAT: a mixture of finely ground raw or cooked meats of various kinds. It is seasoned according to stuffing, mixed with breadcrumbs, cream, and eggs. Usually other foods are stuffed with it. It is also used to make quenelles, sausages, and strudels.

FREE RANGE: any farm animal allowed to roam and feed without confinement.

FROSTING/ICING: normally a sugar-based, boiled mixture used to coat and decorate cakes and other baked goods. It is also an uncooked butter cream and egg-based variation used for filling and coating tortes and cakes.

FUMET: a very concentrated reduced fish, mushroom, or seafood stock. It adds flavor to otherwise bland sauces.

GAME ANIMAL (INCLUDING BIRDS AND REPTILES): a term applied to any living creature in the wild deemed for human consumption. Its distribution is strictly controlled by the Food and Drug Administration.

GARNISH: a decorative accompaniment to a finished dish.

GASTRONOMY: the art and science of fine gourmet dining.

GHERKIN/CORNICHONS: the young fruit of a certain variety of small dark green cucumber. The small fruit is marinated in pickling brine.

GLACE: a stock that is reduced to a syrup-like consistency. Also applies to caramel, fruit infused aromatics, and syrups.

GOURMAND: a connoisseur of fine food and drink.

GRAPE SEED OIL: My preference for use in greasing pans so food doesn't stick. Cooking spray is a perfectly fine substitution.

JULIENNE: to cut food into very thin strips.

MANDOLINE: a compact, hand-operated kitchen tool with various interchangeable blades for thick and thin slicing of solid and firm vegetables. Also an excellent tool to cut juliennes of firm root vegetables.

MARINADES: most marinades consist of acids, wine, vinegar, herbs, and in some cases sugar. Its use is to tenderize and flavor tough cuts of certain meats, especially beef and game.

MASCARPONE: a triple-rich cream cheese from the Lombardy region of Italy. Excellent on its own or in any recipe calling for cream cheese. No tiramisu should be made without this excellent product.

MEUNIÈRE: mainly for fish entrees, such as sole. The fish is lightly dusted with flour, simply sautéed in butter and finished with a dash of white wine, lemon, and parsley.

MIMOSA: a garnish for salads, resembling the yellow mimosa flower. Hard-boiled egg yolks are finely chopped and sprinkled over salad greens, like a dust of pollen from the same flower.

MIREPOIX: root vegetables cut into fine juliennes for roasting bones; designated to create stocks.

MOUSSE: meaning foam or froth. A very rich, airy dish, such as chocolate mousse. Many other dishes refer to this airy and light concoction.

PANADA: a thickening agent consisting of a liquid, flour, and eggs. Used for terrines and pâtés.

PAN-BROIL: to cook uncovered in a skillet without fat.

PAN-COOK: to partially cook by any method.

PAN-FRY: to cook in a skillet with a small amount of fat.

PÂTÉS, GALANTINES, TERRINES: all three types are flavorful, finely ground force meats.

Pâté is a French term for meat pie. They can be baked in ceramic terrines or wrapped in special pie sheets, as "pâté en croûte." Duck, goose, or rabbit galantines are tightly wrapped in cheese cloth and heavy foil and poached rather than baked. They are mainly used as appetizers or snacks.

PAUPIETTE: a thin slice of meat, usually veal, rolled around a seasoned filling, meat, or vegetable. Mostly pan-fried and served with a sauce. Paupiettes are the same as Rouladens.

POACH: to cook food in liquid.

QUENELLES: light, delicate spoon dumplings, consisting of seasoned ground meat, fish, or vegetables that are gently poached in stock.

RICE FLOUR: finely ground, used as a thickening agent in place of regular flour. For people with allergic reactions to regular flour or wheat products.

SAUTÉ: to cook quickly in a small amount of fat.

SCALDING POINT: heat a liquid to just before boiling point.

SEAR: to brown food quickly at a high temperature.

SHOCK: to pour ice water over cooked foods, especially vegetables, to stop the cooking process.

SIMMER: to cook a liquid at a gently bubbling point.

STRUDEL: a type of paper thin pastry, much like phillo, spread with a savory filling, rolled up, egg washed, and baked to a golden color. Filling can vary from meats to fruits to savory ground nuts.

SWEAT: to cook in a small amount of fat over low heat.

TRUSS: to tie poultry into a compact shape for cooking.

ZEST: the grated peel of a citrus fruit. The zest used in the recipes in this book is always finely grated using a microplane.

HIGH-ALTITUDE COOKING

Please keep in mind that at high altitude, because of less air pressure, cooking takes on a different aspect. For example, water will boil at 198 degrees compared to 212 degrees at sea level. Water or any boiling liquid will be cooler by 14 degrees, so a longer cooking procedure will be required. Consider it when boiling potatoes, eggs, rice, beans, even tender vegetables, along with many other food items.

Lower air pressure also causes boiling liquids to evaporate more quickly. This is especially crucial when fixing stocks, cream soups, or delicate sauces. If not properly watched, sauces, soups, and stocks can turn to glue—not a pleasant outlook if it has to be eaten. Among others, syrups, fruit glaces, and caramels take on a new meaning and new techniques. Any reducing liquid needs to be very carefully watched, especially small quantities since they boil faster and also evaporate faster. *They are not cooked and done faster, however.* It is also very important when baking yeast-based items, such as breads, to be mindful that it will take double the time to proof properly. Also, baking temperatures should be decreased by 25 degrees. But again, baking time needs to be increased, otherwise breads may be nicely browned outside, but will still be raw in the middle. This also applies to cake bases containing eggs, chocolate, wet or dry fruits, or any other wet agent.

In thirty years of high-altitude cooking, especially baking, I found it best to accomplish a satisfying goal in the early morning hours, with calm, windless skies and quiet atmosphere, time to meditate, time with God, and also time to bake.

To improve conditions, I normally have a large pot of gently boiling water on the side. Any high-altitude baking on windy and very dry days is, in most cases, a waste of time.

I have baked breads to perfection in these conditions, but many other times I could have sold them as house building bricks.

Handling Fruits and Vegetables

Keep in mind that even fruits and vegetables obtained from organic cultivated farms are handled, even under sanitary conditions, by many hands. Those grown in soil, even though they might be washed many times, may still have soil and sand clinging to them. All fruits and vegetables need to be cleaned under cold running water before using for any human consumption, whether used in stock pots, roasting pans, or any other cooking method.

A word of warning: Any egg yolk and butter-based sauce needs to be made fresh and used as soon as possible, such as Sauce Hollandaise, Sauce Béarnaise, and many of its variations. DO NOT keep them overnight. Also do not freeze them. These sauces are highly prone to food poisoning.

Hummingbirds
There are hummingbirds galore at the Fawn Brook Inn. Mieke has 14 feeders that she fills twice a day, using 75 pounds of sugar a week.

Kara at one of the feeders.

HERBS AND SPICES IN THE KITCHEN

Fresh Herbs

Fragrant, flavorful, and colorful—fresh herbs are by far the most preferred ingredient in cooking. They are very satisfying and fun to be around. They can be grown in a greenhouse, a sunny windowsill, or in the garden. They give foods a very special appeal and deep flavor. They delight our senses and will enhance all aspects of cooking.

Many varieties can also be found in specialty food stores. If properly picked and packed, they will keep their freshness for quite a long period of time in the refrigerator.

When cooking with fresh herbs, one must be aware that a larger amount is needed than if dried herbs are used. Also, most need to be added to the pot at the last minute.

Spices

Man has gathered herbs and spices since long before recorded history. Some were used to banish demons, some to heal sickness, some to purify the air, some to glorify God in the Heavens, and yes, some to even flavor foods. There are many stories in the written Word surrounding herbs and spices, and wars have even been fought over trade routes. Whatever the case, one thing is for sure: it is a great pleasure to use spices in foods, not only as flavorings, but also for health reasons.

They should only be purchased from reliable sources. Avoid supermarkets as these could be quite old and flavorless. Store all spices in airtight containers away from heat and sunlight. Proper storage will not only prolong their vitality, flavor, and color, but will keep their freshness as well.

Spices should not be purchased in large quantities, as most of them have a shelf life of no longer than eight to twelve months, with some exceptions. Also, grain and whole-seed spices have a much longer shelf life than ground and powdered forms. Besides, there is no comparison flavor-wise between a freshly ground seed to a pre-pulverized one.

There is a lesson in each flower,
A story in each stream and bower,
On every herb on which you tread,
Are written words which rightly read,
Will lead you from earth's fragrant sod
To Hope, To Holiness, To God.

—THOMAS OSBORNE DAVIS, 1814–45

Fresh herbs and spices cross stitch was done by Mieke's mother.

HERBS

ANGELICA: A native to the cooler parts of Europe and Iceland. It is also abundant in the higher marshy meadows of the northern and central Rocky Mountains. It's also known as Alexander's or Horse Parsley. The bruised seeds, when boiled in white wine, are very effective for snakebites. Though not of great culinary use, fresh finely chopped leaves added to Sauce Hollandaise are an excellent companion to poached salmon. The stems of the plant can be candied, thus becoming a fine decoration for sweets and desserts. Because of their mild anise flavor, they can be used to enhance preserves, jellies, and marmalades.

BASIL: Several varieties exist. Called by Italians the "Herb of Love," the ancient Greeks looked at it as the "King of Herbs." Its wonderful blend of anise, clove, and mint figures prominently in Greek, Italian, French, and Southeast Asian dishes. It is the main ingredient in pesto and is excellent in fresh salads, egg, and cheese dishes.

CHERVIL: A native to western Asia. The flavor of chervil is fresh, tangy on the tongue, slightly sweet, with a touch of anise seed. In culinary expressions, fine herbs include chervil, parsley, chives, and tarragon. Excellent for omelets, cucumbers, avocados, mushrooms, roasted potatoes, and also to season fish and fowl. Add the leaves at the end of cooking time, as they will lose their delicate flavor with lengthy cooking.

CURRY PLANT: A small upright plant resembling rosemary, with silvery needle-like foliage and beautiful golden-yellow flower clusters. The whole plant finely chopped will give an extra distinctive taste to any curry dish. Use it mixed with lemon grass and parsley on fish and chicken. It is also excellent for seasoning scallops while marinating them in dry champagne, salt, and lime juice. In cooler climates, place the potted plant outside in a sunny location during the summer months. As soon as the first frost occurs, it will do well in a sunny windowsill or greenhouse for the winter. It is quite thirsty, so water it as soon as the soil feels dry. I call this herb a lover's heirloom.

DILL: A native to Russia now found wild and cultivated almost everywhere on this earth. The *Talmud* records that the seeds, stems, and leaves were subject to tithe. It has many uses from pickling to flavoring vegetables, potatoes, sauces, and soups. It goes especially well with grilled and poached fish dishes.

GINGER: A native to the tropical forests of southeast Asia. Introduced by the Romans to Europe, it was a common antidote for the plague. It stimulates gastric juices, and fresh ginger is very soothing for colds and coughs. A slice of the cleansed root steeped in hot water and flavored with a slice of lemon and a dollop of honey will do wonders for congested head-and-chest colds.

The ground form is a must in gingerbread cookies. The crystallized form is excellent for pastries. Freshly chopped ginger will give an extra touch to grilled fish, rice, and chicken dishes. It will also enhance the flavors of curries and chutneys.

To preserve the fresh root, peel off rind, dice the root, and preserve in dry sherry. The sherry is, by the way, also good to drink afterward!

HYSSOP: *Psalm 51:7: "Purge me with hyssop and I shall be clean."* A mixture of crushed peppercorns, thyme, ginger, and anise seed boiled in hyssop syrup will restore the loss of memory.

An herb of ancient times for culinary uses, it is not well known any longer. Its aromatic, slightly bitter flavor is excellent for fish that have a heavy oil content. A few chopped leaves are sufficient to flavor caramels and jellies, and its pretty blue flowers will enhance desserts and salads. This plant comes in many varieties and its flower attracts hummingbirds.

LEMON GRASS: Found in southeast Asia. A fairly new herb to western cuisine, it is an excellent addition to any dish that calls for a tangy taste. Use only fresh products to flavor cream soups, fish, veal, and curry dishes.

LOVAGE: This old-world herb has been well known since ancient times. The Greeks and Romans used it for everything from seasoning foods to remedies of various illnesses. It claims to cure skin rashes, acne, and even stomach pains. However, it is an excellent herb to season roasts, fowl, and enhance any stock or reduction. No bouquet garni should be without this excellent herb. Use the raw leaves in salad as a refreshing taste, or chopped with chives as a final garnish for chicken or beef consommé. It has a very strong celery-like flavor, yet very distinctive on its own. It grows well in cooler climates, and as a matter of fact, the root system needs to be exposed to freezing temperatures to produce well the following season. It can grow up to six or seven feet in height. It grows best when exposed to the eastern sunrise and protected from the afternoon sun and heat. If properly cared for, this herb will grow with you all your life! The French call it Lovage or False Celery, in Switzerland it is known as *Maggikraut,* and in my native Austria is called *Liebstöckel,* the herb of jumping joy.

MARJORAM: A native of North Africa. "A delight to Chefs of Peace and Happiness." This aromatic herb of a thousand uses is a must for any kitchen. It will complement any meat dish. No Christmas goose should be without sweet marjoram and chestnut stuffing. It will also complement green vegetables, soups, and potatoes.

MINT: A universal plant and many varieties exist. The best in the kitchen for culinary use are spear, pepper, and apple mint. A must for the classic rack of lamb with fresh mint sauce. It will add a refreshing taste to chutneys, and gives an interesting touch to mixed fresh salads.

OREGANO: "The joy of the mountains of Greece." A robust Mediterranean herb of spicy fragrance, with a hint of clove and balsam. It is excellent for meatballs, pasta sauces, pizza, gumbo, and pot roast. Oregano is also an excellent salt replacement.

PARSLEY: Flathead or Italian. Cultivated for thousands of years in warm and cooler climates. Legends and superstitions have grown around this herb. It has health-bringing qualities and culinary qualities, the latter being preferred in cooking. It can be used in any variety of dishes, from beef to veal, from fish to fowl, salads, sauces, hot or cold stews, soups, and egg dishes. The list could go on and on. Use it any way you want. It even refreshes plain water and teas. Parsley is also an excellent remedy for people with allergies.

ROSEMARY: "Dew of the Sea" as this fragrant herb is called in Latin. This has a very strong pine needle flavor, so it should be used with caution. Excellent companion to garlic, lamb, and game. No duck should be roasted without it. A fresh sprig steeped in olive oil makes an excellent butter substitute for bread.

SAGE: A medicinal plant, called *Salvia* in Latin, which means "to save." A native to the northern shores of the Mediterranean, it also grows in abundance in our Rocky Mountain West. There can be no better and finer meat than a fresh antelope loin who feeds on the tender sage twigs of Wyoming, or an elk steak from the sagebrush-covered high Colorado mountain ridges. Sage and wild game dishes, needless to say, go hand in hand. Sage is also claimed to be the herb of eternal youth. Even our native wild turkeys feed on sage, and it complements veal and chicken dishes. It is used quite frequently in Italian dishes. This herb is excellent in salt-free cooking.

TARRAGON: A native of southern France, it is the "King of culinary Herbs." Its sophisticated flavor of licorice and pepper will give aromatic fragrance to any kitchen. Because of its extremely potent flavor, it must be used with discretion. It is a must for the "Queen of Sauces"—Béarnaise. It's also excellent for any chicken dish, fish, mustard sauces, and home-made vinegars.

THYME: A native to southern Europe. Its pungent clove-like taste works well on its own or blended with other herbs and garlic. Use in stocks and soups, and on roasts, lamb, and chicken.

SPICES

ALLSPICE: A native of Jamaica. It is a berry that looks much like a peppercorn. To obtain the spice at its best strength, use the whole berry rather than the ground form. They are easily crushed in a mortar and will release an aroma of freshly ground pepper, cloves, and nutmeg. It is

a must for stocks, marinades, and slow-cooking stews. Freshly ground, it will enhance the taste of grilled fish, poultry, meat loaves, and pâté. It can also be used in sweet cakes and pastries.

BAY LEAVES: Native of the Orient. This is the leaf of the laurel tree famous throughout history. *Psalm 37:35: "I have seen the wicked in great power and spreading like a green bay tree."* A laurel wreath was placed on the heads of heroes in ancient Greece and Rome. In modern times, it is an excellent flavor enhancer for any stock, roast, soup, and marinade. The bay leaf has a very pleasing aromatic warm scent and should not be missed in any kitchen.

CARAWAY SEEDS: A native to the cooler parts of Europe. Folklore has it that if caraway seeds are used in cooking, it will prevent infidelity in love. But it also has a variety of culinary uses. They are fabulous in breads and are a must for sauerkraut and cabbage dishes. They will cut the fat content in meat dishes, enhance the flavor in roasted or boiled potatoes, and greatly reduce the smell of garlic on your breath.

CARDAMOM: Native to the Indian subcontinent. There are three varieties of this spice—white, green, and black; the white and green being the more flavorful ones. Since they come in a seedpod, the white and green varieties very seldom split, thus keeping the intense flavors of the seeds. The longest, black cardamom seedpods will crack and the flavor of the seeds will lessen after a period of time. White cardamom is a main ingredient in Scandinavian baking, especially Christmas goods.

CASSIA BUDS: Native to China and North Vietnam. Sweet in aroma with a flowery cinnamon flavor, it's excellent for pickling fruits, compotes, and preserves. Infuse into hot cream or milk to make custards and desserts.

CELERY SEED: A cultivated plant from Europe. Its seeds are used in combination with salt, garlic, and pepper for roasts, especially beef and pork. Their warming aromatic scent also goes well with clear soups, stews, and old-fashioned meat loaf.

CINNAMON: A native to the island of Sri Lanka. The cinnamon of commerce is obtained from the inner bark of the tree. Quills are cut out of the bark and tied into bunches. The Jews valued it highly as a spice and perfume. It was one of the ingredients of Moses' anointing oil as we read in Exodus 30:23–25. Cinnamon is used in many savory dishes, and is a must for apple strudel, hot spiced wine, sweet rolls, puddings, and rice. Its uses in cooking are infinite.

CLOVES: A native to the Molluccas Island. The tree will only grow in tropical climates close to the sea. Bright pinkish-red flower buds are harvested and dried in the sun until they turn brown. Because of the highly scented oil in the flower heads, they should be used with restraint. This is a must for apple pie and hot-spiced wine. Use them in marinades or use an onion studded with cloves in a pot roast. No Christmas ham should be without them. A few smashed cloves will greatly enhance any chicken or beef stock.

CURRY POWDER: A blend of many spices and used in many different ways. It is fun not only to mix your own, but also to try in different foods, from veal to poultry to fish, and in casseroles and on vegetables. It is very important to dry all grains in very gentle heat before grinding them. It will bring out a rich and toasty flavor.

Curry Powder
YIELD: ½ cup

Ingredients
½ oz green cardamom seeds
½ oz fenugreek
¼ oz white peppercorns
¼ tsp mace, flaked
¼ tsp anise seeds
¼ tsp celery seeds
3 whole cloves
Pinch of cayenne pepper
Pinch of freshly grated cassia cinnamon
Few threads of saffron
¼ tsp freshly ground ginger

Procedure
Combine all seeds, including cloves, and toast them very lightly in a hot oven. Grind them in a seed grinder to a fine consistency. Add the cayenne pepper, the cinnamon, saffron, and ginger and combine well.

Note: This curry powder does not have a very long shelf life, so if not used right away, store it in an airtight container in the refrigerator or freezer.

FENUGREEK: A native to the warm climate of the Mediterranean Sea. A very nutritious seed and used since ancient times, the flavor and fragrance resembles that of honey. The seeds should be lightly toasted before grinding. Very tasty in vegetarian dishes, curries, and lamb marinades.

JUNIPER BERRIES: A native to Europe, North Africa, North America, and the Arctic Regions. As they are of a very strong flavor, discretion should be used in flavoring foods with them. Add them to marinades, game dishes, fowl, and stuffing. The berries need to be crushed before use. As they need three years to ripen, turning from yellow-green to blue-black, only choose the soft blue-black berries when picking them in the wild. The juniper needles (very sharp) give excellent flavor to fresh grilled fish, and fresh twigs placed on coals can flavor steaks, sausages, and even hamburgers.

MACE: A native to the Spice Islands. It is now also grown extensively in the West Indies, especially on the Island of Grenada. It is the protective cage-like covering of the nutmeg seed. It is a most precious spice, softer in flavor than nutmeg, greatly enhancing the taste of mashed potatoes, pumpkin pie, clear beef consommé, and steamed vegetables.

MUSTARD SEED: Remember the parable of the mustard seed? This seed is unique among spices and has been treasured as a condiment and digestive stimulant since earliest times. Yellow and brown seeds are available, the yellow ones being sharper in flavor. Coarsely ground, they are excellent in vinaigrette dressings. Ground to powder, it is fun to make your own mustards of various flavors. The seeds are used in marinades, especially sauerbraten, corned beef brisket, and, of course, the most famous dill pickle. For mustard making, use glass, ceramic, or stainless steel containers only. **Never use aluminum.**

NUTMEG: To get its full, pleasantly pungent flavor, it should always be grated fresh. The ground variety will lose its flavor in a very short time. Its spicy warming flavor goes well with cheese dishes. It is a must for cheese fondue, eggnog, soufflés, and quiches. Nutmeg could be acclaimed as the national spice of the Netherlands, for the Dutch use it quite heavily.

PAPRIKA: A native to Central America. A sweet and fragrant spice with a slightly earthy smell, it comes from a specially cultivated pepper, Capsicum, the best coming from Hungary. "Hungarian Rosen Paprika" is by far the best of all the paprikas available. It is an excellent spice for cream sauces, casseroles, chicken, fish, and meat dishes.

PEPPERCORNS: A native to the tropical islands of the East Indies. A spice valued as most precious from earliest times, and in the Middle Ages it was even used as currency from time to time. Its culinary uses are manyfold and it goes well with any other spice or herb. A mixture of all the different peppercorns, cracked in a mortar or ground in a coarse peppermill, will make a "steak au poivre" an unforgettable feast. Freshly ground pepper is also excellent for the digestive system. **All peppers are best when freshly ground.**

BLACK PEPPER: The most commonly used of all the peppers. They are picked from the vine not quite ripe and fully mature. They are then dried in the hot sun, thus making them the hottest tasting one to the palate.

WHITE PEPPER: The fully ripened berries are picked, soaked in water until the outer black shell becomes loose and then it is removed. A cream-colored kernel is exposed, thus making it somewhat milder than its black cousin. This makes it an ideal seasoning for white sauces, fruitcakes, tarts, and even pies. Did you know that in the time of the romantic steam locomotive, only white pepper was used in the train's kitchen? Otherwise passengers would complain of having coal soot in their food!

GREEN PEPPER: A pleasant addition to our modernized cooking techniques. The berries are picked before they are fully ripened. Lightly mashed in a mortar, they will give a light, clean, fresh peppery taste. They are ideal for seafood, poultry, and vegetable dishes. If at all possible, use only freeze-dried berries, as they will retain the best flavor. They can also be used in a peppermill.

PINK PEPPER: Not a true pepper at all, but fun to use in any dish from Nouvelle cuisine to Classical cooking. Their sweet peppery taste will enhance any kitchen and is sure to please any chef. They are excellent in a peppermill and should therefore be freeze-dried.

CHINESE PEPPER: Again, not a true pepper and little known in the Western World, but quite an important spice in the Asian countries, including Russia. The little reddish colored berries are very aromatic and excellent for soups, stews, and fowl.

LEMON PEPPER: Also not a true pepper, but I use it a lot in the kitchen. It's a mixture of freshly ground white pepper and microplaned lemon zest to taste. It can also be purchased.

POPPY SEEDS: One of the oldest spices on record. It is known for its nutritious and medicinal value. This tiny seed is excellent for baking breads and desserts, and for salad dressings. Grind them fine and mix them with buttered noodles for a delicious nutty flavor.

SAFFRON: A native of Asia, but now also cultivated in Turkey, Italy, and Spain. The best now comes from Spain. It is one of the world's costliest spices. Only the orange-colored hand-picked stigmas of a special crocus flower can be used. It takes about 80,000 handpicked stigmas to make 500 grams or about one pound of saffron. It is a slightly bitter, very aromatic spice and should be used very sparingly. It has been a highly prized spice since Biblical times, as we read in *Song of Solomon 4:14: "Spikenard and saffron, calamus and cinnamon ..."* The spice is used for bouillabaisse, paellas, risotto, and many other sauces and dishes.

STAR ANISE: A native of southwest China. Its rich, strong aromatic anise flavor is most fabulous when freshly ground and used in baking. Great for Christmas baking. A few stars will greatly enhance a rib roast if placed below the meat in the roasting pan. One or two stars placed inside a duck during roasting will make a duck dinner most memorable. It will retain its aromatic flavor for a few years if stored properly in an airtight container.

VANILLA: A native of the tropical Americas. The vanilla seedpods were first brought to Europe by the Spaniards as one of the most fragrant of all the culinary spices. This one comes from a most beautiful climbing orchid. It is most precious and flavors custards, cream desserts, cakes, ice creams, and also savory sauces for fish, veal, and fowl. Homemade vanilla sugar is superior to any store-bought extract and is fun to make and to use. When buying vanilla beans, be sure they are of a plump, moist, dark brown consistency. Refuse dried and shriveled-up bean pods.

Edible Flowers

BERGAMOT: Also known as "Indian Plume." Its heads are aromatic and refreshing in cool summer drinks and salads. Its ragged flower heads, when strewn over cold soups, not only give them special accent, but their freshness will also enhance the flavor. It is also great in poultry stuffings when combined with sage and garlic. Member of the Monarda family.

BORAGE FLOWERS: It is said that this little flower brings great courage. Use the flowers when freshly opened in iced tea or white wine, with a few young leaves for an extra refreshing taste. They are very attractive when floating on a cold cucumber-potato soup, and give color to salad greens. Young leaves resemble cucumbers in taste.

CAPER FLOWERS: These short-lived flowers make an excellent plate garnish to any well-prepared food item. The flower buds are picked and pickled and become the well-known capers. The seed heads also come pickled and can be used in cold sauces and salad dressings.

CHIVE FLOWERS: Their delicate flavor will enhance not only vinegar when steeped in it and cured on a sunny windowsill, they are also excellent when picked and strewn over clear beef and chicken broth, white cheeses, salads, and sauces.

CLOVE-SCENTED PINKS: Their deliciously spicy scent makes an excellent garnish for any custard or cold cream containing vanilla. It's also an excellent companion for cold fruit soups such as cherry, apricot, or peach.

LEMON- OR ROSE-SCENTED GERANIUMS: Many varieties exist and not all are suitable for culinary uses. The normally scentless flower heads are just used as garnish. However, the leaves can be preserved in confection sugar and aged, thus the sugar can be used for frostings, baking, flavoring custards, and cold dessert creams. A combination of scented leaves and rose petals give quite a sweet-smelling, fascinating aroma. The leaves combined with fresh orange zest make an excellent nerve-calming tea.

NASTURTIUM: A native of Peru. The flowers and leaves with their peppery taste are an excellent addition to salads. The unopened buds can be pickled and used as a caper substitute, however, do not use large quantities of the caper-like berry, as they can become quite a nuisance to the stomach.

PANSIES AND JOHNNY JUMP-UPS: Excellent for garnishing hors d'oeuvres, salads, cooling summer drinks, and cold dessert creams.

POT MARIGOLDS: The bright orange varieties are the best ones for culinary uses. Scatter the petals with their distinctive piquant flavor over salads, cream soups, rice, and creamy white cheeses.

SWEET VIOLET: The newly opened flowers that have a very delicate flavor are an excellent garnish to cold cream soups, attractive in salads, infused in sugar syrup, and will flavor ice cream toppings and puddings. *Leaves are not recommended for eating.*

SWEET WOODRUFF: Not very well known in our land, this sweet smelling and cheerful herb makes a fabulous garnish for any berry-based cream, or just a few tiny leaves and its star-shaped flower heads as garnish on fresh berries will make them a royal treat. Sun-dried bunches make an excellent herb tea, and sweetened with honey will not only soothe, but also refresh, your battered nerves.

WILD FIREWEED FLOWERS: Those sweet smelling pink flower heads will enhance any refreshing summer salad.

WILD ROSE PETALS: Try these delicately scented petals fresh in salads or even on sandwiches, and are excellent when used with apple glaze for fruit tarts. Rose hips, very rich in vitamin C, make excellent nutritious syrups and jellies, and are a very rare but welcome winter treat on any frosty cold day.

ZUCCHINI FLOWERS: A gourmet's delight. Use only freshly picked flowers and carefully check them for insects. Dip them in beer batter and deep-fry them to a golden color. Serve with sauce rémoulade or piquant cocktail sauce.

Mieke and her flowers.

SUBSTITUTES FOR CERTAIN FLAVORING COMPONENTS

CURRY: The list of curry powder is endless. It's up to your taste to make your own as outlined in this book. It is great fun and extremely satisfying.

DILL, FENNELL: Fresh feathers of either one can be used in cream soups or refreshing cold sauces. Dill is more pungent; fennel is sweet with a hint of licorice.

ELEPHANT GARLIC: Milder and less pungent.

GARLIC: No substitute for this unique bulb.

GINGER: Fresh, crystallized, or powdered. There is no substitute for freshly grated ginger in various cooking methods. Freshly grated, dried, and pounded in a mortar to a powder will do wonders in curries and cookies.

LEEKS, GREEN ONION, CHIVES: Can be interchanged if one or the other is not available, but keep in mind that leeks are milder than green onions, and chives are much finer in taste than leeks or scallions.

LOVAGE: Celery root is the closest in flavor and taste.

MAYONNAISE: No substitute exists. If you have eggs, a good olive oil, and fresh lemon or lime juice, it is a joy to make your own and a taste treat above anything.

MINT: Many varieties exist; use your own taste buds and imagination.

MSG: God did not invent it, nor do I use it. It is simply a slow working poison.

MUSTARD: So many varieties exist, it is impossible to name them all. It is most simple and rewarding to make your own.

OREGANO, MARJORAM, BASIL: All three are interchangeable in various cooking methods if used fresh and with discretion.

PARSLEY, CHERVIL, TARRAGON: Parsley, broad leafed or curly, is unique on its own. Chervil is delicate and sweet, licorice tasting. Tarragon can be interchanged for one or the other, however, discretion in various uses is greatly advised.

SAFFRON: There is absolutely no substitute for the taste, texture, and color of this most precious of all spices.

SHALLOTS: Mild and sweet, only Maui onions or Georgia's famous Vidalia onions would come close in taste.

March 2003.

Christmas Eve

An unseen benefit of growing up at the Fawn Brook was that the restaurant was open for every holiday, which meant that we generally got to celebrate a day early, when the restaurant was closed. Christmas Eve was always a special occasion. Mom and dad would fix a special meal for the family, which I now know involved more work than I could then appreciate. After dinner we would light the final candle on the Advent Wreath, and open our presents. I was very aware that all of my friends were just dying for the night to end so they could open their presents, but there I was, half a day early enjoying the same with my family.

I still appreciate this time we had together, as do my parents. Now that my sister and I live in corners far from home, my parents open the Fawn Brook to the greater Allenspark community each Christmas Eve. I have returned home for far too few of these Christmas Eves, but when I do, I cherish each one.

The gardens at the Fawn Brook Inn are an oasis for birds. In the summer a multitude of hummingbirds enjoy the flowers, and in the winter many varieties of birds feast on numerous types of feeders.

Above: Alex and Cayden.
Left: Opa and Cayden.
Bottom: Opa and Alex.

Stocks and Reductions,
Hot Sauces, Cream Sauces,
Butter Sauces, Glaces, Syrups,
and Flavored Butters

Stocks

Standard Recipe for Mirepoix
(root vegetables cut into fine juliennes for stocks)

3 oz carrots	2 oz celery
3 oz leeks	2 oz garlic
2 oz lovage	4 oz onion
2 oz turnips	4 oz tomatoes

Chicken Stock

YIELD: 8 cups

Ingredients

1 cup grape seed oil

2 lbs chicken, cut into small pieces,
 bones and skin included

1 standard recipe mirepoix (above)

1 standard recipe bouquet garni (above right)

½ cup coarse kosher salt

12 cups water

4 cups Madeira wine

Procedure

Place chicken parts in roasting pan, coat them with the grape seed oil and roast in a preheated oven at 485 degrees for 30 minutes. Sprinkle ¼ cup salt over chicken parts and roast for another 30 minutes. They should be nicely browned on all sides.

Place chicken parts into a stock pot, cover with water and bring to a boil. Reserve the roasting pan with the oil for the mirepoix. As soon as the stock boils, reduce the heat and simmer. Place the mirepoix in the roasting pan and place it in the hot oven for 30 minutes. Sprinkle the remaining salt over the vegetables and roast until al dente. Pour the Madeira over the vegetables and roast another 20 minutes. Carefully place them into the stock pot with the chicken. Add the bouquet garni.

Bring back to a boil, reduce heat and simmer for about 3 hours or until the liquid is reduced to about half of its original volume, about 8 cups. Strain the stock through a fine wire-mesh sieve. Cool it in an iced water bath before placing in refrigerator for future use.

Standard Recipe for Bouquet Garni
(tied in double-lined cheesecloth)

½ tsp crushed white peppercorn

½ tsp crushed allspice

½ tsp cloves

1 tsp chopped lemon grass

1 tsp mustard seed

Sprig of lovage

3 crumbled bay leaves

2 sprigs parsley

2 sprigs rosemary

2 sprigs thyme

Dark Veal Stock

Use approximately 4 lbs veal bones, knuckle, and marrow bones. Brown well in roasting pan and proceed as for chicken stock.

Beef Stock

Use beef knuckles, marrow bones, and oxtails. Proceed as for chicken stock.

Wild Game Stock

Use elk, venison bones, etc. Add fresh sage and crushed juniper berries to bouquet garni and proceed as for chicken stock.

Duck, Pheasant, Goose, and Turkey Stock

Duck: Add caraway seeds to bouquet garni

Pheasant: Add lavender to bouquet garni

Goose: Add marjoram to bouquet garni

Turkey: Add lemon grass and sage to bouquet garni

Proceed as for chicken stock.

HOT BROWN SAUCES
(Basic sauces used for making other sauces)

Sauce Espagnole
YIELD: 6 cups

Ingredients
2 quarts dark brown veal stock (pg. 20)
2 cups Madeira wine
2 cups tomato juice
1 cup grape seed oil
1 lb chicken meat, finely diced
2 oz garlic, finely diced
4 oz leeks, chopped fine
8 oz ripe tomatoes, chopped fine
Roux (see below)

Procedure
In a saucepan, combine veal stock, Madeira, and tomato juice, and bring to a boil. In a skillet, heat the oil, add the chicken and garlic, and lightly brown the meat. Add the leeks and lightly sauté. Add the tomatoes and heat thoroughly. Carefully incorporate into the stock and bring back to a boil. Reduce heat and simmer until reduced to about half its original volume (about 1½ hours). Carefully incorporate the roux to the finished sauce.

Roux
Rice flour is used in all recipes calling for roux as a precaution for the many people who are allergic to wheat products. The roux can be used for either brown or white sauces.

Ingredients
¼ cup grape seed oil
½ cup rice flour

Procedure
In a skillet, heat oil and slowly add the flour. Over low heat and constant stirring, cook the rice flour until a light golden color is achieved. Carefully incorporate the roux to the finishing sauce. Lightly whisk sauce until roux is completely dissolved. Simmer sauce for about 15 minutes more. Pass finished sauce through wire-mesh sieve. A word of caution: because of the roux, the sauce easily burns. A gentle simmer and frequent stirring is necessary.

Glace de Viande
YIELD: 1 quart

Ingredients
1 quart dark veal stock (pg. 20)
1 quart beef stock (pg. 20)

Procedure
Place the stocks in a heavy saucepan and bring to a boil. Reduce the heat and gently simmer for 3½ hours, longer if needed, skimming off all fat and scum as it accumulates on the surface. It should be reduced to half its original volume. Strain the finished product through a fine wire-mesh sieve. Place into a shallow container, refrigerate until completely set. Slice it into small 8-ounce squares and refrigerate or freeze until future use.

Demi-Glace
YIELD: 2 cups

Ingredients
1 cup Sauce Espagnole (left)
½ cup dark veal stock (pg. 20)
8 oz Glace de Viande (above)
½ cup dry sherry

Procedure
Combine all ingredients in a heavy saucepan. Mix well and bring to a boil. Reduce heat and gently simmer the sauce for about 30 minutes, whisking on occasion so as not to burn it. Strain through wet cheesecloth.

Madeira Sauce
YIELD: 2 cups

Ingredients
2 cups Demi-glace (above)
1 cup Madeira wine

Procedure
In a heavy saucepan, add the Demi-glace and Madeira wine and gently simmer for about 30 minutes, or until the sauce is reduced to about 2 cups.

Black Truffle Sauce

(also known as Sauce Périgueux)
YIELD: 1 cup

Ingredients

1 cup Madeira Sauce (pg. 21)
½ cup Sauce Espagnole (pg. 21)
1 Tbsp truffle essence
1 Tbsp black truffle oil
1 tsp black truffle, finely chopped

Procedure

Combine sauces, truffle essence, and oil and very gently simmer the sauce for about 45 minutes or until reduced to about 1 cup. At the very end, stir in the chopped truffles.

Game Sauce

YIELD: 1½ cups

Ingredients

In a mortar, combine and pound to a coarse consistency:

6 whole allspice berries
6 plump juniper berries
4 whole cloves
6 white peppercorns

1 Tbsp black truffle oil
2 oz shallots, finely diced
1 oz diced garlic
1 Tbsp fresh sage, chopped
1 cup fine port
Zest of 1 small orange, plus the juice from the orange
1 cup game stock (pg. 20)
1 cup Madeira Sauce (pg. 21)
4 oz fresh berries (blueberries, blackberries, currants, etc.)

Procedure

In a saucepan, combine shallots, garlic, and sage with the truffle oil and very lightly sauté. Add the pounded spices and herbs; add the port, orange juice, and game stock. Gently simmer and reduce the liquid to about ½ cup (liquid should look like syrup). Gently incorporate the Madeira Sauce, and continue to simmer the sauce for about another 20 minutes. Add desired berries and orange zest at the last minute.

Sauce Cumberland

YIELD: 4 servings

Ingredients

1 cup port
½ cup Cointreau liqueur
¼ cup orange juice
¼ cup lemon juice
1 Tbsp shallot, finely minced
Zest of ½ orange
Fine juliennes of ½ lemon (flesh and zest)
1 cup Apple Glace (pg. 29)
½ Tbsp English mustard
1 Tbsp ginger root, peeled, chopped very fine
½ cup red currants or lingonberries (well drained if frozen)
Dusting of cayenne pepper

Procedure

In a heavy saucepan, combine port, Cointreau, orange and lemon juice, shallots, orange zest, and lemon juliennes. Set over high heat and bring to a boil. Reduce heat and gently simmer until reduced to half its volume. Strain the liquid and add the Apple Glace, mustard, and ginger. Bring back to a simmering point and reduce to about 1 cup. Place into a container, stir in the drained berries, season with the cayenne pepper, and cool before using.

NOTE: this can also be made into aspic by adding gelatin. In a skillet, heat ½ cup verjus (page 32), then dissolve 1 tablespoon gelatin in liquid. When completely dissolved, add to Sauce Cumberland, then pour into a tray and refrigerate until completely set. Use a shaped cookie cutter (such as a leaf) to cut pieces of aspic to be used as garnish for Game Pâté.

Hot White Sauces

Fish Glace

YIELD: 4 cups

Ingredients

2 lbs white fish meat
1 recipe Mirepoix (pg. 20)
2 oz sliced mushrooms, preferably Shiitake
¼ cup kosher salt
1 small lime, quartered
8 cups water
4 cups dry white wine
1 recipe bouquet garni (pg. 20)
4 egg whites
½ tsp kosher salt
¼ cup plain gelatin
3 oz grated carrots

Procedure

In a saucepan combine mirepoix, fish, mushrooms, ¼ cup salt, and lime. Cover with water and wine. Bring to a boil over high heat; reduce heat and simmer for 1 hour. Add the bouquet garni and continue simmering for another 1½ hours. In a bowl, whisk egg whites with ½ tsp salt. Slowly add gelatin, and lastly fold in the grated carrots. Set aside. Strain stock through a fine wire-mesh sieve. Return to heat, whisk in the egg whites and carrots. Bring back to boil, reduce heat and gently simmer for 45 minutes. *Do not disturb stock during final simmering time.* Again, strain through cheesecloth into a shallow container. Refrigerate until well set; cut into 4-ounce squares. Wrap and freeze or refrigerate for future use.

Thermidor Sauce

YIELD: 4 servings

Ingredients

1 cup Sauce Béchamel (above)
½ cup cream sherry
¼ cup crème fraîche (pg. 25)
Dusting of nutmeg

Procedure

Combine all ingredients except nutmeg and bring to a boil. Reduce heat and gently simmer for about 20 minutes. Finish sauce with a dusting of nutmeg.

Sauce Béchamel

YIELD: approximately 2 cups

Ingredients

1 small shallot
1 clove of garlic, finely chopped
1 Tbsp Dijon mustard
1 sprig parsley
1 sprig thyme
¼ tsp mace
Pinch of coarse sea salt
1 bay leaf, crumbled
1 star anise
5 allspice berries, crushed
5 cracked white peppercorns
5 whole cloves
2 cups chardonnay wine
2 cups heavy cream
4 oz Fish Glace (left)
¼ cup grape seed oil
¼ cup rice flour
Dusting of cayenne pepper

Procedure

In a saucepan combine shallot, garlic, mustard, and all seasonings except cayenne pepper with white wine. Bring to a boil. Reduce heat and simmer, reducing it to half its volume. Gently add the cream and fish glace. Bring back to a boil and again reduce heat and simmer, reducing to half its volume. Simmering time is approximately 1½ hours. In separate skillet, heat the oil, add the rice flour and over low heat make a smooth roux, being careful not to burn it. Carefully combine the roux with the cream. Gently whisk the sauce until roux is well incorporated. Finish the sauce with just a slight dusting of cayenne pepper. Gently simmer the sauce for another 15 minutes. Strain the sauce through a fine wire-mesh sieve.

Mornay Sauce

YIELD: 4 servings

Ingredients

1 cup Sauce Béchamel (pg. 23)
½ cup crème fraîche (pg. 25)
Pinch of cayenne pepper
1 large egg yolk
¼ cup Swiss or Gruyere cheese, grated
Dusting of nutmeg

Procedure

Combine Sauce Béchamel, crème fraîche, and cayenne pepper. Bring to a boil and reduce heat. Whisk in egg yolk and grated cheese. Gently simmer for about 20 minutes. Dust with nutmeg to finish sauce.

Saffron-Curry Sauce

YIELD: 4 servings

Ingredients

1 cup Sauce Béchamel (pg. 23)
½ cup heavy cream
½ cup crème fraîche (pg. 25)
2 sprigs of curry plant
1 Tbsp crystallized ginger
1 tsp Madras curry powder
Pinch of saffron

Procedure

Combine Sauce Béchamel, cream, and crème fraîche. Bring to a boil and reduce heat. Incorporate curry sprigs, ginger, curry powder, and saffron. Gently simmer sauce for about 30 minutes. Remove the sprigs of curry plant.

Vanilla-Saffron Sauce

YIELD: 4 servings

Ingredients

½-inch long vanilla bean
1 cup Sauce Béchamel (pg. 23)
½ cup crème fraîche (pg. 25)
¼ cup heavy cream
Pinch of saffron
Dusting of freshly grated nutmeg

Procedure

Immerse the outside of the vanilla pod into vanilla sugar (page 150). Slice the vanilla bean lengthwise and scrape the inside of the pod. In a saucepan, combine all ingredients except nutmeg. Bring to a boil. Reduce the heat and gently simmer the sauce for about 30 minutes. Finish the sauce with just a dusting of freshly grated nutmeg. This sauce is a must for jumbo sea scallops.

Sauce Beurre Blanc

YIELD: approximately 4 servings

Ingredients

2 oz shallots, finely diced
½ oz garlic, minced
1 Tbsp parsley, chopped
¼ cup balsamic vinegar
2 cups champagne
¼ cup dry white wine
1 cup heavy cream
¼ lb unsalted butter,
    softened to room temperature
2 Tbsp smooth Dijon mustard
2 Tbsp drained capers

Procedure

In a saucepan, combine shallots, garlic, and parsley with the balsamic vinegar, champagne, and wine. Bring to a boil. Reduce heat slightly and simmer until reduced to ¼ cup. Slowly incorporate the cream. Bring back to a slow boil and again reduce the heat. Gently simmer the sauce for about 10 minutes. Gradually add the butter, making sure it is completely melted before adding more. Strain the sauce immediately through a fine wire-mesh sieve. Very gently stir in the mustard and capers. Add salt and pepper to taste. *A word of caution:* this sauce will separate and break if kept too hot for too long.

COLD CREAM SAUCES

Mayonnaise
YIELD: 1½ cups

Ingredients
6 large egg yolks
½ tsp sea salt
¼ cup extra virgin olive oil
1 Tbsp fresh lime juice
1 tsp balsamic vinegar
1 tsp smooth Dijon mustard
Dusting of nutmeg
Dusting of cayenne pepper

Procedure
In a mixing bowl, add salt to the egg yolks and beat until thick and lemon colored. Reduce the speed and very slowly add the olive oil; beat until well combined. Slowly incorporate the lime juice and vinegar. Add the mustard and seasonings; add a little salt if needed.

A word of caution: This sauce curdles very easy. The cause is that the oil is too cold or added too fast, or surrounding area is too hot. Prepare it in a cold place and all utensils should be cold. If it curdles, place a tablespoon of boiling water in a bowl and under constant stirring add the sauce drop by drop.

Saffron-infused Mayonnaise
YIELD: 1½ cups

Add approximately ¼ tsp of saffron threads to the mayonnaise recipe above. Serve on the side.

Sauce Tartar
YIELD: 1½ cups

Ingredients
1 cup mayonnaise (above)
½ cup crème fraîche (right)
4–5 chives, finely chopped
2 small cornichons, finely chopped
1 Tbsp capers, finely chopped
4–5 parsley sprigs, chopped
½ hard boiled egg, finely chopped

Procedure
Combine all ingredients and mix well.

Crème Fraîche
YIELD: 1 cup

Ingredients
1 cup heavy cream
1 Tbsp buttermilk

Procedure
In a stainless steel pot add the cream, then stir in the buttermilk. Set over a gentle heat and gently bring the cream to 85 degrees. Remove from heat and pour mixture into a glass, ceramic, or stainless steel container. Cover with plastic wrap and let it stand in a warm place, 65–70 degrees, for 24 hours. Refrigerate for another 12 hours, or until well thickened, before using.

Sauce Remoulade
YIELD: 1½ cups

Ingredients
1 large filet of anchovy
1 cup mayonnaise (left)
½ cup crème fraîche (above)
4–5 chives, finely chopped
4–5 parsley sprigs, chopped
2 small cornichons, finely chopped
½ oz celery heart, finely chopped

Procedure
In a bowl, chop up the anchovy and puree it with the back of a spoon. Combine all ingredients and mix well.

Curry Sauce
YIELD: 1½ cups

Ingredients
1 cup mayonnaise (left)
½ cup crème fraîche (above)
2 oz shallots, finely chopped
1 oz ginger, freshly grated
Few threads of saffron
Dusting of freshly grated nutmeg
½ oz curry powder
Grated fresh coconut for garnish

Procedure
Combine mayonnaise and crème fraîche; add all seasonings and mix well. Sprinkle sauce with the freshly grated coconut.

Roasted Pimiento–Ginger Sauce

YIELD: 3 cups

Ingredients

3 Tbsp olive oil
1 small clove of garlic, minced
7 oz pimiento (roasted red pepper)
2 Tbsp chives, chopped
1 tsp lemon grass, chopped
1 cup mayonnaise (pg. 25)
¼ cup fresh ginger, peeled and chopped
¼ cup capers, drained
1 Tbsp verjus (pg. 32)
1 Tbsp lime juice
¼ tsp salt
¼ tsp sugar
Dusting of ground cinnamon
Dusting of cayenne pepper

Procedure

Place olive oil and garlic in a skillet over high heat to quickly roast the garlic. Carefully add pimientos and cook them until the skin is lightly scorched. Add chives and lemon grass. Mix well and remove from heat. In food processor, combine mayonnaise, ginger, capers, verjus, and lime juice; pulse to mix. Add all seasonings, the pimiento, and the herbs and oil from skillet. Puree to a fine consistency and check for correct seasoning. Sauce should have just a little bite to it. Add more salt and cayenne if needed.

To Roast and Peel Peppers

Have a brown (not lined or sprayed) paper bag ready. Quarter the pepper and remove all the seeds and membranes. Place the quarters skin side up in a pie tin greased with grape seed oil. Place tin in preheated 500 degree oven until the skin starts to blister, about 15 minutes. Remove from the oven and place the pepper quarters into the paper bag and close tight. After 5 minutes, remove the peppers from the bag and carefully peel the skin away. Trim off burned parts.

Dill Sauce

YIELD: 1½ cups

Ingredients

1 cup mayonnaise (pg. 25)
½ cup crème fraîche (pg. 25)
1 shallot, about ½ oz, finely chopped
4–5 sprigs of chervil, finely chopped
5–6 dill feathers, finely chopped

Procedure

Combine all ingredients and mix well.

Honey Mustard

YIELD: approximately 6 oz

Ingredients

8 oz ground English mustard
½ tsp salt
3 oz scented vinegar (pg. 32)
3 oz dry white wine
2 Tbsp fine honey

Procedure

Combine mustard, salt, vinegar, and wine; incorporate well. Mix in the honey. Pour into a glass or ceramic jar, cover with a tight fitting lid, and cure the mustard in a warm, but not hot, place for about 4 weeks.

NOTE: DO NOT use a corrosive or aluminumbased pot to store and cure the mustard!

Mustard Sauce

YIELD: ¼ cup

Ingredients

2 Tbsp smooth Dijon mustard
2 Tbsp scented vinegar (pg. 32)
1 tsp granulated sugar
Pinch of rock salt
3 Tbsp extra virgin olive oil
Dusting of chopped dill

Procedure

Whisk together mustard, vinegar, sugar, and salt. Continue to whisk and slowly incorporate the oil. Season with dill.

BUTTER AND EGG-BASED SAUCES

THIS CLASS OF SAUCES includes five basics, including Hollandaise, Béarnaise, Choron, Maltaise, and Mouseline. These are all rich sauces and require the following basic understanding and principles. None of these sauces is thickened with flour, but with a liaison of egg yolks and butter. If properly made, they are a delight to anyone's taste buds. Great care must be taken with vinegar, juice-based reductions, or stewed-related items because they need to be reduced properly and kept warm. Butter has to be melted down and clarified and kept warm. Egg yolks must be beaten over a light simmering water bath. If they are not heated slowly and gradually, they will become granular and can turn to scrambled eggs. Also, the melted clarified butter must be added very slowly and by continuous whisking into the egg yolks. The sides of the bowl need to be scraped as you whisk, otherwise the egg yolks will continue to cook and get very gritty. As soon as the butter is completely incorporated into the sauce, remove it as quickly as possible from the heat source. Carefully whisk in the required ingredients. Keep the finished sauce in a warm place and use as needed as soon as possible. *None of these sauces should be refrigerated or kept over.* These sauces, if not properly handled and used, can be a great cause for salmonella poisoning.

TO CLARIFY BUTTER: Use unsalted butter and over high heat melt, evaporating most of the water and separating the milk solids, which sink to the bottom of the pan, leaving a golden liquid on the surface. Remove from heat and let it rest for about 30 minutes. Skim any foam off the top, and carefully ladle the cooled butter into another container without disturbing milk and water solids. Discard the milky residue in the bottom of the pan.

TO BEAT EGGS OVER A LIGHT SIMMERING WATER BATH: A double boiler may be used for this purpose, or by placing a container (pan, bowl, etc.) *over* a pan filled with hot water. *It is important that the pan containing the eggs never touches the water.* This technique is designed to cook delicate dishes without breaking or curdling them.

YIELD FOR THE FOLLOWING FIVE SAUCES IS FOR 4 SERVINGS.

Each of these sauces can be used for various veal, chicken, or fish dishes. Some are also excellent on certain vegetables, such as steamed asparagus, Belgian endive, broccoli, cauliflower florets, etc.

Sauce Hollandaise

Ingredients
¼ lb butter
3 large egg yolks
1 Tbsp fresh squeezed lemon juice
½ tsp sea salt
Pinch of cayenne pepper

Procedure
Melt and clarify the butter; keep it warm. Whisk the eggs over a simmering water bath until thick and creamy. Carefully and slowly whisk in the warm butter. When well combined, add the lemon juice, salt, and cayenne to taste.

Sauce Béarnaise
"The Queen of a fine butter sauce"

Ingredients
2 Tbsp scented vinegar (pg. 32)
1 Tbsp shallots, finely minced
½ tsp chervil, chopped
4 white peppercorns, crushed
½ tsp sea salt
¼ lb butter
3 large egg yolks
½ tsp chopped fresh tarragon

Procedure
Combine vinegar, shallots, chervil, peppercorns, and salt. Over low heat, reduce to half its volume. Let it cool. Melt and clarify the butter; keep warm. Whisk eggs over simmering water bath until thick and creamy. Carefully and slowly whisk in the warm butter. As soon as sauce is done, remove from heat. Strain the vinegar mixture with a fine wire-mesh sieve and carefully whisk into the sauce. Incorporate the tarragon. Taste for correct seasoning, add more salt if needed. Sauce Béarnaise is a must for Eggs Benedict.

Sauce Choron

Ingredients

    1 recipe Hollandaise –
       NO CAYENNE PEPPER (pg. 27)
    1 Tbsp olive oil
    2 oz Roma tomatoes, skinned,
       de-seeded, and chopped
    1 tsp chives, minced
    1 tsp parsley, minced
    ¼ tsp lemon pepper (pg. 13)
    ½ tsp fresh basil, optional

Procedure

Place olive oil in a skillet. Combine tomato, chives, parsley, and lemon pepper and lightly sauté just enough to heat the tomato all the way through. Mash mixture with a fork to a fine pulp and gently incorporate into the Hollandaise. For a refreshing flavor, chop in ½ tsp fresh basil.

TO SKIN AND SEED TOMATOES

Bring very lightly salted water to a boil. With a small paring knife, remove stem core from fruit. Make a crosswise incision and carefully plunge the fruit into the boiling water. Poach it for about 2 minutes or until skin comes loose. Remove from hot water and cool in a pan of iced water. Gently take cooled fruit into your fist with removed core-side facing down, and gently squeeze out the seeds.

Sauce Maltaise

Ingredients

    1 recipe Hollandaise (pg. 27)
    1 tsp zest of blood orange
    ¼ cup fresh juice of a blood orange

Procedure

Combine zest and juice over low heat; reduce to half its volume. Gently incorporate with Sauce Hollandaise.

Sauce Mouseline

Ingredients

    1 recipe Hollandaise (pg. 27)
    ¼ cup fresh whipped cream (pg. 149)

Procedure

Just before serving, gently fold the whipped cream into the Hollandaise.

Adrieke and Kajetan, both at the age of two.

GLACES AND SYRUPS

Apple-Raspberry Sauce

YIELD: about ½ cup

Ingredients

2 lbs firm hard apples, coarsely chopped
with core and seeds
1 cup super fine sugar
8 oz fresh raspberries
¼ cup freshly squeezed lime juice
2 cups water, enough to cover apples

Procedure

Combine apples, sugar, raspberries, lime juice, and water. Bring to boil, reduce heat and simmer until apples turn mushy. Add more water if needed.

Drain apples through a double-lined wire-mesh sieve until all liquid has been extracted. It should yield about ¾ of a cup of liquid. Bring the liquid back to a boil, reduce the heat and gently simmer the liquid for about 35–40 minutes until the glace starts to thicken. It should achieve a honey or syrup-like consistency.

Rose Petal Scented Syrup

YIELD: 1 cup

Ingredients

1 lb sugar   2 oz. dry rose petals
2 cups water   1 glass jar with lid
¼ cup lime juice

Procedure

Use only rose petals that have not been exposed to any insect spray or other poison. Check carefully for crawling bugs, etc. Place petals on wire screen and place in a sunny and airy, moist-free place to dry.

Combine sugar, water, and lime juice and bring to a boil, continuously stirring with a wooden spoon until the sugar is dissolved. Reduce heat and simmer stock down to 1 cup. Place dried rose petals in glass jar, and pour the hot syrup over the rose petals. Seal the container and let it rest in a dark, cool place for about 8–10 days. Drain all liquid off the rose petals, squeezing out as much liquid as possible. Discard rose petals. Pour the liquid into a glass bottle, seal it, and refrigerate. Do not use a metal container to store the finished product!

Apple Glace

YIELD: 1 cup

Ingredients

2 lbs tart apples, chopped coarsely,
core and seeds included
2 cups water, enough to cover apples
¼ cup fresh lime juice
½ cup Calvados brandy
1 cup fine sugar

Procedure

Place apples in saucepan and cover with water. Simmer until they start to turn to mush—do not let the water evaporate, add more if needed. Drain the apples through a double-lined wire-mesh sieve. It should yield about ¾ cup of liquid. Add the lime juice, Calvados, and stir in the sugar. Set over heat and bring to boiling point. Reduce the heat and gently simmer for about 45 minutes to 1 hour, until glace starts to thicken to the consistency of honey.

Apple-Raspberry-Pepper Glace

YIELD: about ½ cup

Ingredients

1 recipe Apple-Raspberry Sauce (left)
1 Tbsp chipotle pepper, finely chopped,
including seeds

Procedure

The amount of peppers should be to taste. Combine the peppers with the glace and heat slowly over low heat. Add more peppers if it's not hot enough. End product should be like thick honey.

Raspberry Mint Sauce

YIELD: 2 cups

Ingredients

2 cups Apple Glace (above)
10 oz fresh raspberries
⅓ cup white crème de menthe

Procedure

Combine all three ingredients in a saucepan. Set over a moderate heat and gently simmer for about 1 hour, or until reduced to about 2 cups. Pass the sauce through a food mill fitted with the smallest blade and remove all raspberry seeds.

FLAVORED BUTTERS

BUTTER, JUST LIKE OILS AND VINEGARS, can be flavor-enhanced with many edible flowers, leaves, herbs, and also orange, lemon or any other citrus zest, for example.

Nasturtium Butter

YIELD: 4 servings

Ingredients

4 oz unsalted butter
2 Nasturtium flower heads
1 Nasturtium leaf

Procedure

Bring butter to room temperature. Place butter in a mixing bowl and whip until double in volume. Carefully chop the flowers and leaves to a coarse consistency—do not bruise them too much. Fold into whipped butter. Place butter into a pastry bag fitted with a small star tube and pipe butter out in 4 equal-sized rosettes. Refrigerate to harden butter.

Garlic Butter

YIELD: 1 lb

Ingredients

1 lb unsalted butter
½ tsp kosher salt
1 Tbsp firmly packed minced garlic
1 tsp parsley, chopped
½ tsp fresh thyme leaves
1 tsp chives, chopped
Dusting of freshly ground white pepper

Procedure

Bring butter to a very soft stage at room temperature. In a bowl, combine all ingredients except the butter, and mix well. Place butter into a mixing bowl and beat at high speed until butter doubles in volume. Reduce speed and slowly incorporate all seasonings. Mix until well combined. Place butter in refrigerator until somewhat hardened. Form four equally long sausage-type rolls; wrap in parchment paper and then in plastic wrap. Refrigerate or freeze and use as needed.

Lemon Butter

YIELD: 1 lb.

Ingredients

1 lb. butter
Zest of 2 lemons

Procedure

Bring butter to a very soft stage at room temperature. Place butter into a mixing bowl and beat at high speed until butter doubles in volume. Reduce speed and slowly add zest. Mix well. Place butter in refrigerator until somewhat hardened. Form four equally long sausage-type rolls; wrap in parchment paper and then in plastic wrap. Refrigerate or freeze and use as needed.

Almond Butter

YIELD: 1 lb.

Ingredients

1 lb. butter
½ cup almonds

Procedure

Bring butter to a very soft stage at room temperature. Place butter into a mixing bowl and beat at high speed until butter doubles in volume. Reduce speed and slowly add almonds. Mix well. Place butter in refrigerator until somewhat hardened. Form four equally long sausage-type rolls; wrap in parchment paper and then in plastic wrap. Refrigerate or freeze and use as needed.

Trout pond

Vinegars,
Salad Dressings,
Concentrated
Herbal and Spiced Oils

Fruit-scented or Spiced Vinegar

YIELD: 2 cups

Ingredients

½ cup well-packed berries—raspberries, blackberries, blueberries—you make the choice
1 cup vinegar
1 cup dry champagne
Zest of 1 medium size lemon

Procedure

Pack a clear glass bottle or container with the berries, and add the vinegar to it. In a saucepan, combine the wine with the lemon zest and bring to a fast boil. Immediately remove from heat source; let it cool a little, then add it to the vinegar and berries. Seal the bottle with a tight-fitting lid or cork. Set in a sunny windowsill and cure it for about two weeks, gently shaking the bottle several times during curing procedure. If the cork becomes too loose, a wax or plastic seal is highly recommended.

Flavor the vinegar to your liking with your choice of fruit, fresh herbs, or a variety of de-seeded roasted peppers, garlic, chives, etc.

Verjus

YIELD: 4 cups

Ingredients

½ lb green, unripe grapes with seeds
Juice of 1 lime (about 1 Tbsp)
1 bottle (750 ml) dry sparkling white wine

Procedure

Slice grapes in half and lightly smash them. Place into a glass jar, including seeds. Season with lime juice and cover tightly with a lid and plastic wrap. Let it rest in a cool place for two days. Add the sparkling wine to it, seal the container off tightly and let it cure for two weeks in a cool, but not cold, place. Refrigerate as soon as seal is broken. Replenish with more wine as depleted, until grapes turn to mush. Strain the mushy grapes and re-use liquid for next batch.

SALAD DRESSINGS

Vinaigrette

YIELD: 2 cups

Ingredients

Large clove of garlic (about 1 oz), finely minced
2 large anchovies, finely chopped
½ cup extra virgin olive oil
1 Tbsp scented vinegar (left)
1 Tbsp balsamic vinegar
1 Tbsp smooth Dijon mustard
½ tsp salt
Dusting of freshly ground white pepper
¼ cup fresh berries of your choice

Procedure

In a bowl, combine the minced garlic and anchovies. With the back of a spoon, smash them well to form a paste. With a whisk, slowly incorporate the oil. Add the vinegars and mustard. Combine ingredients well. Season to taste with the salt and pepper and add the berries.

Apricot-Lemon Vinaigrette

YIELD: 4 servings

Ingredients

1 cup apricot liqueur
¼ cup dry white wine
1 Tbsp rose petal syrup (pg. 29)
2 Tbsp lemon juice
Zest of medium lemon
½ cup lemon oil (pg. 36)
Salt and pepper to taste

Procedure

In a saucepan, combine liqueur and white wine. Over low heat, simmer until reduced to ½ cup, being careful that liquid does not ignite if an open gas flame is used. In a bowl, combine the rose petal syrup, lemon juice, and the zest. Add mixture from saucepan. Whisk in the lemon oil, season with salt and pepper to taste. Add a few more drops of lemon juice if so desired. This is the perfect dressing for romaine hearts. Garnish the salad with avocados, star fruit, and tomato wedges.

Balsamic Vinaigrette

YIELD: 4 servings

Ingredients

½ cup extra virgin olive oil
⅓ cup balsamic vinegar
1 tsp fresh lime juice
1 tsp sugar
1 tsp garlic, minced
1 tsp chives, minced
Pinch of salt
Pinch of lemon pepper (pg. 13)

Procedure

Whisk together the oil, vinegar, lime juice, and sugar. Add the garlic and chives. Season with salt and lemon pepper to taste.

NOTE: This vinaigrette can be interchanged in various ways: Nut infused oils can be used; substitute honey for sugar, and orange juice for lime juice—flavors can vary to one's liking. Add a berry taste by steeping berries in balsamic vinegar for several days, such as raspberries, black berries, blueberries, etc. Let it age in bottles in a sunny windowsill.

Lemon Oil Dressing

YIELD: 1½ cups

Ingredients

6 large egg yolks
¼ cup lemon oil
1 Tbsp balsamic vinegar
1 tsp lime juice
1 tsp Dijon mustard
1 Tbsp smashed anchovies
1 tsp garlic, finely minced
½ tsp salt
½ tsp lemon pepper
Dusting of nutmeg

Procedure

Beat the egg yolks until thick and creamy and slowly incorporate the lemon oil until combined well. Whisk in the vinegar, lime juice, mustard, and anchovies. Add all the seasonings and mix well. The dressing should stay creamy and thick. Coat crisp romaine hearts with the dressing and serve with a dash of Roquefort cheese.

FAWN BROOK FAMILY MEMORIES

Caesar Salad

Anyone who has visited the Fawn Brook and has been fortunate enough to order the Caesar Salad, then to be further blessed by having it prepared table-side by my mom, has been given a gift to please their palate like never before. My husband and I have been married for fifteen years and he still doesn't understand why I didn't inherit any of the cooking genes from my parents. His favorite Fawn Brook experience is my mom's salad. Last time we were home, my mom made him this incredible salad and finally, after all these years, shared her wisdom and explained step by step how to create it. Still, to this day, we have not been able to duplicate the taste. So, although my dad was fortunate to make a memorable Caesar Salad for the astronauts in Houston, my mom can claim this one as her masterpiece!

Caesar Dressing

YIELD: 4 servings

Ingredients

1 medium clove of garlic
2 anchovy filets
2 Tbsp extra virgin olive oil
½ tsp smooth Dijon mustard
Fresh juice of ½ lime and ¼ lemon
Dash of Worcestershire sauce
Dash of Tabasco Sauce
Dusting of freshly ground pepper
1 large egg
Grated parmesan cheese
Seasoned croutons
1 head of romaine lettuce
freshly grated parmesan cheese for garnish

Procedure

This vinaigrette is best prepared in a wooden bowl. In a wooden bowl, chop the garlic and the anchovies, and with the back of a spoon smash them well to form a paste. Slowly incorporate the oil and mustard. Drizzle in the lemon and lime juice. Add the Worcestershire sauce and Tabasco Sauce. Place the egg in hot water for ten seconds to curdle the white. Crack the egg, discard the white, and swiftly whisk the yolk into the dressing. Add the romaine leaves and coat them well with the dressing. Place the salad on chilled plates and garnish with freshly grated parmesan cheese and pepper. Accompany salad with freshly seasoned toast points (page 47).

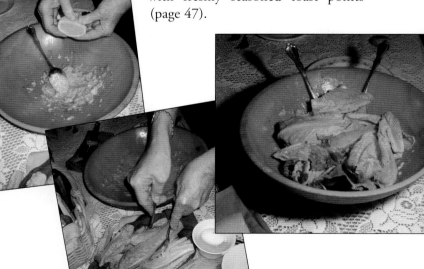

Herbal and Spiced Oils

ALL HOMEMADE OILS should be prepared with great care to prevent contamination and also food poisoning. Containers, glass jars, or bottles need to be properly sterilized, cleaned, and dried. *Metal containers are not recommended or safe!*

Do not fill liquid all the way to the top of container—a ⅛-inch gap should be allowed. Bottles and jars need to be properly sealed and stored. Seal with either wax or strong plastic tape. Store containers in a cool and somewhat darker corner of the kitchen, away from sunlight and heat. Once opened, refrigerate containers. Properly close off and use up as soon as possible.

Not all oils are suitable for use in a home kitchen because of their heat resistance. Recommended oils are: grape seed oil, peanut oil, sunflower oil, and canola oil. For reasons of safety, olive oil is not recommended for the following recipes because of its low resistance.

All oils for the following recipes need to be heated to 325 degrees, then cooled down depending on flavoring agent. All flowers, leaves, or herbs from the garden should not have been exposed to any insecticide or any other poisonous spray. Before use, gently rinse all flowers, herbs, or leaves in cold water. Dry on paper towels and inspect for "hiding" insects inside flower heads.

Recommended flowers are: nasturtiums plus leaves, begonia flowers, violets, monarda flower petals, wild rose petals, pot marigold petals, Johnny Jump-up's, and herbs.

Roasted Garlic Oil
YIELD: 8.45 fl oz (250 ml)

Ingredients
9 oz grape seed oil
1 oz elephant garlic, finely diced
1 tsp sea salt flakes

Procedure
In a skillet, combine oil, garlic, and salt. Set over high heat and roast garlic until nicely browned on all sides. The oil needs to heat to 325 degrees. As soon as garlic is toasted, remove from heat and cool before filling container. Seal properly and cure for about one week, away from sunlight and heat. Refrigerate after opening.

Roasted Pimiento-Rosemary Oil
YIELD: 8.45 fl oz (250 ml)

Ingredients
2 oz red and golden oven-roasted pimientos
8½ oz grape seed oil
1 tsp sea salt flakes
Sprig of fresh rosemary

Procedure
Roast pimientos (page 26); julienne to fine strips. Combine oil and salt in skillet and heat to 325 degrees. Very carefully add julienned pimientos. Sear for just a few seconds, add the sprig of rosemary at the last second and remove from heat source. Cool oil down before filling container. Insert pimientos and rosemary into container before adding oil. Seal properly and cure for about one week away from sunlight and heat. Refrigerate after opening.

Lemon Oil

YIELD: 8.45 fl oz (250 ml)

Ingredients

9 oz grape seed oil
1 tsp sea salt flakes
1 Tbsp lemon zest

Procedure

In a skillet, combine oil and salt. Heat to 325 degrees. Remove from heat. Cool oil down to about 250 degrees and whisk in the lemon zest. Cool oil down a little more before filling container. Seal container and cure for one week away from sunlight and heat. Refrigerate after opening.

Nasturtium Oil

YIELD: 8.45 fl oz (250 ml)

Ingredients

1 large nasturtium leaf
2 nasturtium flower heads
9 oz grape seed oil
1 tsp sea salt flakes

Procedure

Julienne the nasturtium leaf and place in a skillet; add the flower heads, then add oil and sea salt. Heat to 325 degrees. Remove from heat and cool down to about 200 degrees. Fill container and seal. Cure for about one week away from heat and sunlight. Refrigerate after opening.

Oma and grandson Cayden cooking together.

Appetizers

Pâtés and Terrines

All pâtés are prepared with the finest of "Highly Seasoned Force Meats"; they can be of fowl, seafood, game, and other meats, or even vegetables. Some can be baked in pastry casings, others are surrounded with fatty substances. In most cases they are poached. If a terrine or pâté mold is used, simply place prepared force meat in mold according to recipe, cover with lid and aluminum foil and place into poaching vessel. Fill the poaching vessel one-quarter full with boiling water, cover with lid and follow poaching instructions in recipe.

If a loaf pan is used and a simple container for poaching, double wrap the loaf pan with aluminum foil, securely sealing the ends so no steam or liquid can penetrate into the pan. Put a metal screen or a double-folded heavy kitchen towel in the bottom of the poaching pan to prevent scorching the pâté. Again, fill poaching pan one-quarter full with boiling water, seal loaf pan airtight with aluminum foil and poach according to recipe.

PÂTÉS AND TERRINES

All of the following recipes call for a 2-cup capacity mold or loaf pan.

Pie Pastry for Pâté en Croûte

YIELD: enough for a 2-cup terrine mold

Ingredients

¼ tsp salt

3 oz all-purpose white flour, sifted

4 oz unsalted butter, cold and cut into small cubes

1 small egg

Procedure

Combine salt and flour, and with a fork quickly mix in the butter cubes. Mix until all butter is well combined with the flour. Mix in the egg and work the dough until a smooth elastic paste is achieved. Add a dusting of flour if needed. Dust hands with flour and form a smooth ball. Wrap dough in plastic wrap and refrigerate for about two hours.

On a flat, lightly floured surface, roll the dough out to about ⅛-inch thickness. Line a sheet pan with parchment paper, place dough on it, cover with plastic wrap and refrigerate until needed.

Use the pastry for Pâté en Croute or any other meat pie. Generously brush the terrine mold with grape seed oil (or you may use cooking spray) and dust the bottom and sides with flour. Press the dough into the mold, extending slightly above the rim. Trim off excess and reserve the trimmings for the top. Place the meat mixture into terrine. Roll the trimmings out to ⅛-inch, lightly brush the dough with cold water, place dough on top and press to seal. Cut two small holes in the pastry top to allow steam to escape. Decorate the top with dough leafs, brush with egg wash (pg. 3), and bake in preheated oven at 375 degrees for 15 minutes. Reduce the heat to 350 degrees and bake for another 45 minutes. The top should be golden brown. Completely cool before unmolding.

Pâté en Croute is dry baked according to recipe. DO NOT PUT PÂTÉ EN CROUTE INTO A WATER BATH!

The pâté can be unmolded as soon as it can be handled, however it must be done carefully. You may need to loosen the sides with a knife.

Three-Layer Vegetable Terrine

YIELD: 4–6 servings

Ingredients

4 6-inch long, thinly sliced carrot strips

Salted water

2 9-inch long, thinly sliced English cucumber strips

Lemon juice

Grape seed oil

2½-inch wide pimiento strips

4 oz artichoke hearts

4 oz water chestnuts

4 oz roasted pimientos

¼ tsp cayenne

1 tsp crème de menthe (green)

Pinch of saffron (about 3 threads)

½ cup heavy cream

1 large egg yolk

¼ tsp salt

1 Tbsp gelatin

Procedure

Lightly poach carrot strips in salt water, just long enough to make them flexible. Rinse them in cold water. On a tray, lay out cucumber strips and carrot strips. Very lightly sprinkle them with salt and lemon juice. Cover them with plastic wrap and cure them for a short time (about 30 minutes).

Lightly brush a 2-cup terrine mold with grape seed oil, or use cooking spray. (If canned vegetables are used, drain them well of all liquid.) Place the roasted pimientos, artichoke hearts, and water chestnuts in separate bowls. Season roasted pimientos with cayenne pepper and puree in a food processor to a medium coarse consistency. Season artichoke hearts with the green crème de menthe and again puree to a medium coarse consistency. Slice and season chestnuts with saffron and puree. Keep the three purees separate. Line the bottom and sides of the terrine mold alternately with cucumber strips and carrot strips (reserve 2 carrot strips for the top). Extra lengths of cucumber strips will hang over outside of mold.

Place cream in a skillet. Add salt and egg yolk. Swirl the yolk and combine it well with the cream. Lightly heat the cream. DO NOT LET IT BOIL! Carefully dissolve gelatin in it. Whisk equal amounts into each of the three vegetable purees and combine well.

Place water chestnut mixture in bottom of terrine, pressing mixture down firmly so no air pockets remain. Place pimiento strips down the center and let the mixture stand for a few minutes; then proceed with the artichoke mixture in the same manner. Again let it stand for a few minutes. Mixture should be set but not firm to the touch. Top the terrine off with the pimiento puree and again let it set for a little while. Place 2 carrot strips over the terrine and fold over the cucumber strips. Firmly wrap the terrine with plastic wrap and refrigerate for about 12 hours before unmolding.

Country-Style Game Pâté

YIELD: enough for a 2-cup terrine mold

Ingredients

Seasoning for pâté. In a nut grinder, grind to a fine consistency:

¼ tsp clove	½ tsp chives
¼ tsp allspice berries	¼ tsp mace
¼ tsp cinnamon stick	Dusting of cayenne pepper
¼ tsp coriander seed	¼ tsp salt
6 oz duck or game meat	1 large egg
2 oz goose or duck liver	¼ cup heavy cream
2 Tbsp orange vodka	¼ cup pistachios
1 oz white bread, crust removed and cubed	1 tsp chopped black truffle
1 Tbsp black truffle oil	½ cup Madeira wine
1 Tbsp garlic, minced	1 tsp plain gelatin
½ tsp parsley, chopped	4 dried apricots, split length-wise
½ tsp thyme leaves	Grape seed oil

Procedure

Cut out one 5-inch long (finger thick) strip of meat. Cube the rest of the meat and liver and marinate it with the orange vodka for four hours. Place cubed bread in skillet and sprinkle it with the black truffle oil. Place over medium heat to lightly toast it. Add the chopped garlic, parsley, thyme, chives, mace, cayenne, and salt. Remove from heat. In a bowl, whisk egg and cream together, then combine with the bread mixture. Let it rest for about 30 minutes.

Drain meat and liver of all liquids and place in a food processor. Add the ground pâté seasonings and bread mixture. Chop it to a medium consistency: DO NOT OVER PROCESS IT! Place contents into a bowl and fold in the pistachios and black truffle. In a skillet, heat the Madeira, dissolve gelatin in it, and mix with the force meat.

Brush terrine mold with grape seed oil or cooking spray and fill it half full with the force meat, pressing down firmly so no air pockets remain. Place apricots down the center, place the strip of meat over them, and finish with the rest of the force meat, again pressing down to avoid air pockets. Brush top of terrine with grape seed oil and double wrap with aluminum foil and place terrine in a hot water bath. Cover with a lid or foil and poach in a preheated oven at 375 degrees for 1 hour and 15 minutes. Remove from hot water and cool completely before unmolding.

Smoked Salmon Terrine

YIELD: enough for a 2-cup terrine mold

Ingredients

8 oz smoked salmon, sliced

10 oz mascarpone

½ tsp salt

1 tsp parsley, finely chopped

1 tsp chives, finely chopped

1 tsp dill, finely chopped

1 tsp lemon grass, finely chopped

¼ tsp lemon pepper

1 Tbsp toasted pine nuts

2 Tbsp verjus (pg. 32)

1 Tbsp lemon extract

½ tsp plain gelatin

grape seed oil

Procedure

Brush terrine mold with grape seed oil or use cooking spray. Line bottom and sides of mold with sliced salmon, letting part of the slices hang over the rim. Reserve one slice, about 4½ inches long. In a bowl, combine mascarpone with all seasonings and incorporate well. Fold in toasted pine nuts, and set aside. In a skillet, combine verjus and lemon extract. Lightly warm, add and completely dissolve gelatin. Quickly incorporate into the mascarpone mixture.

Fill mold ¼ full with mascarpone mixture, pressing down firmly so no air pockets remain. Tightly roll up length-wise the extra piece of salmon and place it in the terrine. Add the rest of the mascarpone mixture. Tightly fold over the salmon pieces; wrap the terrine with plastic wrap and refrigerate for about 12 hours. Carefully unmold terrine onto a tray. To slice terrine, use a sharp, hot, wet knife.

Kajetan and Jason

FAWN BROOK FAMILY MEMORIES

Kajetan, Jason, and the fish

One of the great things about growing up in a five-star restaurant is not knowing that you reside in one, or what the standards of decorum are. My father had an epiphany one spring and decided that he would begin to serve fresh Colorado rainbow trout during the summer season, with the gardens in front of the Fawn Brook transformed into a cascading series of pools and streams where the trout lived.

For reasons that are still not entirely clear to me, I was asked one evening to catch a trout out of the large pond in the aspen grove near the restaurant. My best childhood friend, Jason Daniels, was spending some time at our home, and went out to the pond with me. It did not take long before we had successfully hooked our catch. Our instructions seemed simple enough: go catch a trout and bring it to your father. So with the first half of our task completed, we moved to the second.

Jason and I were both keenly aware of the premium my father placed on timeliness, and not wanting to waste any time, we took the most direct route from the pond to the kitchen—right through the middle of the main dining room. Just us, a pole, and a trout on the line.

I can only imagine the delight of the customers at witnessing this sight . . . and the horror of my parents at the thought of facing bankruptcy over this unorthodox method of food preparation!

Crayfish-Crabmeat Terrine

YIELD: 4 servings

Ingredients

6 oz crayfish tails, cooked and cleaned

4 oz King crab meat

1 oz white bread, crust removed and cubed

1 Tbsp olive oil, plus a sprinkle to brush mold

½ Tbsp each of chopped chives, garlic, parsley, and thyme

1 large egg

1 cup heavy cream

1 Tbsp fresh ginger, peeled and chopped

½ tsp salt

Dusting of cayenne pepper

Dusting of nutmeg

5 plump heads of cloves, crushed

1 Tbsp verjus (pg. 32)

1 Tbsp balsamic vinegar

¼ tsp gelatin

Procedure

Line a 2-cup terrine mold with parchment paper and brush with olive oil. Set aside 2 tablespoons crayfish tails. Combine the rest with the crab meat and set aside. Place cubed bread in a skillet. Sprinkle with olive oil and lightly roast it on all sides. At the last minute, add the chopped chives, garlic, parsley, and thyme. Place mixture into a bowl and set aside.

In a separate bowl, mix the egg and cream, then combine it with the bread. Let mixture rest for about 15 minutes. Add ginger and all seasonings to crayfish-crab mixture, then combine with the bread. Place in a food processor and chop it to a coarse consistency. Place mixture into a bowl and mix in the reserved crayfish tails. In a skillet, heat the verjus and balsamic vinegar. Dissolve the gelatin in it and briskly mix it into the pâté mixture.

Place the mixture into the mold, pressing down firmly to prevent air pockets from forming. Double wrap with aluminum foil and place terrine in a hot water bath. Cover with a lid or foil and poach in a preheated oven at 400 degrees for 1 hour and 15 minutes. Remove from hot water and cool completely before unmolding.

Lobster-Crabmeat Terrine

Proceed as for Crayfish Terrine above. Use lobster claw meat instead of crayfish tails.

Smoked Trout Terrine

YIELD: 4 servings

Ingredients

1 oz white bread, crusted removed and cubed

1 Tbsp olive oil, plus a sprinkle to brush mold

½ tsp each chopped chives, parsley, garlic, dill, and lemon grass

¼ cup heavy cream

1 large egg

¼ tsp mace

Dusting of cayenne pepper

Zest of 1 small lime

12 oz boneless, skinless smoked trout

2 Tbsp verjus (pg. 32)

1 Tbsp lime juice

½ tsp gelatin

Procedure

Line a 2-cup terrine mold with parchment paper and brush with olive oil. Cube bread to fine croutons. In a skillet, lightly toast croutons with the olive oil. Add the chopped chives, parsley, garlic, dill, and lemon grass and just lightly sweat. Place crouton mixture into a bowl and add in the cream and egg. Season with the mace, cayenne pepper, and lime zest. Let it rest for about 30 minutes.

Chop trout filets by hand to a very coarse consistency and add to the crouton mixture; combine well. In a skillet, heat the verjus and lime juice. Dissolve the gelatin in it and briskly combine with the trout mixture. Immediately place mixture into the mold, pressing it down firmly so no air pockets can form. Wrap tightly with aluminum foil and refrigerate for 8 to 12 hours before unmolding.

Smoked Trout Terrine

Gravlax

YIELD: 4 servings

Ingredients

½ cup fresh squeezed lemon juice

2 Tbsp roasted garlic oil

2 lbs fresh salmon, skin and bones removed

1 tsp coriander, finely ground

1 tsp dill, chopped

1 tsp salt

1 tsp white pepper, freshly ground

1 tsp granulated sugar

Procedure

Combine lemon juice and garlic oil and rub the whole salmon with it. Combine all seasonings and rub into the whole filet also. Place filet on a tray and tightly cover it with several layers of plastic film. Weigh it down with a wooden board and place several heavy weights on it. Keep under proper refrigeration for 5–6 days before serving. Slice the Gravlax very thin and serve with mustard sauce and skillet-browned garlic toast points (pg. 47).

Seafood Remoulade

YIELD: 4 servings

Ingredients

4 oz cooked baby langoustines (prawns)

4 oz poached lobster medallions

2 oz cooked King crab meat

2 oz marinated sea scallops (pg. 103)

1 cup Sauce Remoulade (pg. 25)

4 large boiled shrimp, butterflied

Lemon garnish and red Belgium endive leaves

Procedure

Combine langoustines, lobster, crab meat, and scallops. Generously coat with Sauce Remoulade. Garnish with butterflied shrimp, lemon, endive leaves, and other garnishes to your liking.

Seafood Remoulade

Lobster Remoulade

Same recipe as Seafood Remoulade above, substituting lobster meat instead of seafood variation.

Baked Brie

YIELD: 4 servings

Ingredients

6 oz puff pastry (pg. 64)

8 oz ripe Brie, cold

Egg wash (pg. 3)

Apple-Raspberry-Pepper Glace (pg. 29)

2–3 chopped sundried tomatoes (optional)

Procedure

Roll puff pastry out to a 7 x 9-inch rectangle, plus a little extra for leaf designs. From the edge of the rectangle, cut out 3 small decorative leaves and set aside. Place cold brie on pastry and wrap it, being sure no holes are poked into pastry. Place wrapped brie on a well-oiled cookie sheet with seams to the bottom. Garnish with pastry leaves.

Egg wash and bake in preheated hot oven at 485 degrees until pastry takes on a nice golden hue, about 15–17 minutes. Serve pepper glace warm on the side. For extra flavor, chop 2–3 sundried tomatoes to a coarse consistency and mix it with the warm glace.

The Origin of Steak Tartar

The Tartars were northeastern Europeans living along the Baltic seashore, their main occupation being fierce warriors. In 500 A.D. they started moving southwest and invading other tribal territories, killing, burning, and ransacking settlements in the then vast empty spaces of Eastern Europe, going as far south as the once mighty Roman Empire.

Legend has it that as they galloped on horseback in their travels they would gather seeds and herbs such as wild onions, garlic, mustard seeds, and other wild growing herbs. I imagine they would make a concoction of these herbs and spices and thus marinate the wild meat supply they carried in their knapsacks to make it tender and flavorful.

Another version has it that they would place the cut of meat between the saddle and the horse until it became tender enough to eat "raw as it was"! Well, this is the story of the Steak Tartar as handed down years ago by my teachers and trainers.

I, for one, am glad we now live in a more civilized and enlightened society and can enjoy this delicious morsel of food in a more fashionable and healthier way.   —Hermann

Beefsteak Tartare

YIELD: 2 servings

Ingredients

1 large clove of garlic
2 large anchovy filets
½ Tbsp shallots, finely minced
1/2 tsp capers, mashed
Dusting of sweet Hungarian paprika
1 large egg yolk
Small seedless lemon wedge
1/2 oz Cognac
Dash of Tabasco Sauce
Dash of Worcestershire sauce
8 oz lean beef filet, chopped fine
Freshly ground black pepper, to taste
Pumpernickel bread or warm toast points (pg. 47)

Procedure

In a wooden bowl, hold the garlic with a fork and shave the garlic with a sharp knife. Generously season the bowl by rubbing the garlic around the bowl. Mash the anchovies with the garlic to a fine paste using the back of a spoon. Incorporate the shallots, capers, and paprika. Whisk in the egg yolk, a few drops of lemon juice, and the cognac. Incorporate the Tabasco and Worcestershire sauce to taste. Add the beef to the seasonings, combine it well and finish with freshly ground black pepper. Enjoy the tartare with pumpernickel bread or warm toast points.

Christmas community lunch.

Escargots en Croûte

YIELD: 1 serving

Ingredients

3 oz wood mushrooms, such as morels, shiitake, etc.

8 large Helix Brand cooked snails

½ cup loosely packed garlic butter (pg. 30)

1 Tbsp olive oil

7 oz puff pastry (pg. 64)

Egg wash (pg. 3)

Procedure

Place mushrooms in a casserole dish measuring about 4 x 4 inches and 1/2-inch deep. Distribute the snails evenly around the mushrooms. Top with garlic butter and oil.

Roll out the puff pastry to a rectangle 9 x 7 inches, plus extra for leaf designs. Lightly wet the rim of the casserole dish with cold water and place puff pastry over it, sealing off the edges of the dish well. Flatten out left-over pastry and cut out 3 or 4 leaf designs. Egg wash the pastry and decorate with the leaves. Place dish on a baking sheet and bake in a preheated oven at 500 degrees for 15 minutes or until pastry is puffed up nicely and golden brown.

Escargots need to be consumed immediately!

Wood Mushrooms en Croûte

Prepare and proceed as for Escargots (above), leaving out the snails and increasing the amount of mushrooms depending on appetite.

Sauteed Wild Mushroom Medley

YIELD: 2 servings

Ingredients

2 oz garlic butter (pg. 30)

2 oz wild mushrooms, sliced

½ cup sundried cherries

1 Tbsp chives, chopped

1 oz cream sherry

1 tsp crème fraîche (pg. 25)

2 toast points

Procedure

Place garlic butter in a skillet and bring to a bubbling point. Add the mushrooms and cherries and sauté just until tender. Add the chives, stir well and drain off grease. Return skillet to heat and flame with sherry. Stir in crème fraîche and serve over toast points (see below).

Skillet-Roasted Toast Points

Slice a French baguette into ½-inch thick slices. In a skillet, heat garlic butter and very lightly brown the toast points.

Tropical Fruit Chutney

YIELD: 4 loosely packed cups

Ingredients

⅓ cup fruit-scented vinegar (pg. 32)

1½ cups dry white wine

½ cup brown sugar, loosely packed

1 smoked chipotle pepper

6 whole cloves

2 star anise

1 3-inch long cinnamon stick

1 bay leaf, crumbled

1 papaya, peeled, de-seeded, and diced into bite-size chunks

1 mango, peeled and diced into bite-size chunks

1 cup pineapple, diced

1 star fruit, diced

½ banana, quartered and sliced

2 oz ginger root, peeled and finely minced

1 Tbsp lemon grass, very finely chopped

Procedure

Combine vinegar and white wine in a saucepan. Add brown sugar, chipotle pepper, cloves, anise, cinnamon stick, and bay leaf. Set over medium heat and stir until all sugar is dissolved. Bring to a boil; reduce the heat and gently simmer until reduced to half its original volume.

In a separate saucepan, combine papaya, mango, pineapple, star fruit, and banana. Mix in ginger and lemon grass. Using a wire-mesh sieve, strain the vinegar/wine mixture, and pour over the fruit. Bring it to a boiling point, then reduce heat and gently simmer until fruit is tender. DO NOT BOIL UNTIL FRUITS ARE MUSHY. Refrigerate the chutney for 24 hours before using it.

Soups

The Fawn Brook Inn

HOT CLEAR SOUPS

Chicken Consommé

YIELD: 5 cups

Ingredients

6 cups chicken stock (pg. 20)

2 cups dry sherry

1 lb chicken meat, julienned

1 small piece of garlic, crushed

Sprinkle of olive oil

1 small onion (about 3 oz.), spiked with 6 whole cloves

1 celery heart tied together with 3 sprigs parsley
and 1-inch long lemon grass

¼ tsp salt

4 large egg whites

4 oz carrots, grated

Procedure

Place chicken stock and sherry in stock pot. Set over high heat and bring to a boil. Season chicken with garlic. Sprinkle the chicken with olive oil and place in a skillet and lightly brown on all sides. Combine with the stock and bring to a boil. Reduce heat, add the onion and tied herbs, and simmer stock for 1 hour and 15 minutes. In a bowl, add salt to the egg whites and whisk to a frothy consistency. Combine with the grated carrots. Remove the herb bundle and onion from the stock and gently incorporate the egg whites. Without disturbing, gently simmer the stock for about 45 minutes, being sure the stock does not boil. Carefully strain the consommé through a fine wire-mesh sieve.

Kajetan, age 8, and Adrieke, age 5.

Beef Vegetable Broth

YIELD: 4 servings

Ingredients

3 oz small beef cubes

Sprinkle of olive oil

½ oz garlic, minced

Dusting of nutmeg

3 cups beef stock (pg. 20)

1 cup Madeira wine

2 oz onions, finely diced

1 oz carrots, small cubes

1 bay leaf

1 oz parsnips, small cubes

1 oz leeks, inside whites only, finely diced

2 oz tomatoes, chopped

For Garnish

¼ cup parsley, chopped

¼ cup parmesan cheese, grated

Toasted croutons (pg. 64)

Procedure

Sprinkle beef cubes with olive oil and place in a stock pot. Add the minced garlic and lightly brown the meat on all sides. Dust with freshly grated nutmeg. In a bowl, combine the beef stock and wine and add to the browned meat. Add the onions, carrots, bay leaf, and parsnips. Reduce the heat and gently simmer the soup until the vegetables are just tender. Add the leeks and tomatoes to the pot and simmer the soup just long enough to heat the tomatoes through. Serve garnished with parsley, croutons, and sprinkle parmesan cheese over soup.

Chicken noodle soup

**FAWN BROOK
FAMILY MEMORIES**

Are you ready for some football?

It's hard as a mother to describe how my childhood was so vastly different from my children's because of growing up in the restaurant business. To my oldest son, it seems like a dream to be surrounded by food twenty-four hours a day, and with Opa always there to cook for him. But I have dampened this dream by telling him stories of a certain professional Colorado football team that used to grace our tables several times over the years. My son's bedroom is covered in orange and blue and he dreams of one day becoming a member of the Broncos. For many years these players would have celebrations at my parents' restaurant, and my brother and I would take anything we could find for these athletes to autograph—Christmas cards, napkins, even matchbooks. As a child, these autographs became yesterday's news, but as an adult and a faithful fan, I kick myself daily for not knowing what happened to these mementos.

My dad tells the story of one particular player who requested that his select cut of meat be cut up as hamburger and served with ketchup. Unfortunately for my brother and I, we never saw our sports heros as a team in our home again, but for my dad, his fine cuisine was never again mistaken for "hamburger meat."

Oxtail Soup

YIELD: 4 servings

Ingredients

2 lbs oxtails, cut to 1 inch lengths

½ lb bacon, chopped

½ cup olive oil

2 medium onions, diced

2 small leeks, sliced

2 medium tomatoes, chopped

4 oz garlic, minced

¼ cup kosher salt

½ cup sage, chopped

8 cups water, divided

Bouquet garni, tied securely in cheesecloth:

   Few sprigs of thyme and parsley

   1 tsp whole cloves

   1 tsp allspice berries

   1 tsp white peppercorns

   2 bay leaves

1 cup port

2 cups Madeira wine

3 egg whites

Pinch of salt

3 oz carrots, grated

Chopped chives for garnish

Procedure

Combine oxtails and bacon in roasting pan. Pour the olive oil over it and roast in hot oven at 500 degrees until oxtails are very well browned, about 45 minutes. Add all the vegetables and sprinkle salt and sage over it. Stir everything into the meat and continue roasting for 15 minutes. Carefully add 3 cups of water. Keep in oven until water starts to boil, about 45 minutes.

Remove from oven and place everything in stock pot, scraping out all burned-on food particles. Add 5 cups of water and bring to a boil. Reduce heat, add the bouquet garni and simmer the stock for 4 hours. Strain the stock through a fine wire-mesh sieve, reserving the cooked oxtails. Add the port and Madeira and bring back to a simmering point. In a bowl, beat egg whites with a pinch of salt until peaks form. Combine with the grated carrots and add it to the simmering stock. Continue simmering for another 45 minutes. Line a wire-mesh sieve with a wet cheese cloth and slowly strain the stock. Remove all grease as it accumulates from stock. Check for correct seasoning and add salt if needed. Remove all meat from oxtails, discarding fatty substance. Chop meat to a fine consistency and make quenelles out of it (see recipe for Duck Meat Quenelles, page 68). Serve the soup with the quenelles and garnish with chopped chives.

Goulash Soup

YIELD: 4 servings

Ingredients

- 3 oz bacon, diced
- 2 Tbsp garlic butter (pg. 30)
- 1 oz garlic, minced
- 2 oz onions, minced
- ½ oz green onions, diced
- 12 oz beef, good quality, cubed
- ¼ tsp kosher salt
- 2 oz pimientos or red peppers, coarsely chopped
- ½ oz red tomatoes, chopped
- 2 cups dry white wine
- Bouquet Garni, tied securely in cheesecloth:
    - 1 bay leaf, crumbled
    - 3 white peppercorns
    - 4 whole cloves
    - 4 whole allspice
    - 4 juniper berries
    - ¼ tsp whole caraway seeds
    - (Crack all berries slightly in a mortar)
    - 2 sprigs of thyme
    - 3 sprigs of parsley
- 2 cups beef stock (pg. 20)
- 2 Tbsp paprika
- Light dusting of cayenne pepper
- 1 cup heavy cream
- 2 cups crème fraîche (pg. 25)

Procedure

In a saucepan, brown bacon in garlic butter until crisp. Add minced garlic, onions, and green onions to it and just slightly sweat. Season beef cubes with salt and add to bacon mixture. Nicely brown meat on all sides. Add pimientos and tomatoes, stirring well and keep on very low heat. In a saucepan, add bouquet garni to white wine and bring to a fast boil. Reduce heat and simmer until wine is reduced to half its volume. Add beef stock and bring back to a boil. Meanwhile, dust the browned meat with the paprika and cayenne pepper. Mix well and add the cream to it. Bring to a low boil, reduce heat and keep at simmering point. Remove bouquet garni from beef stock. Add stock to the goulash and mix well. Finish the soup off with crème fraîche. Keep the soup simmering on low heat until meat is tender, about 15 minutes. Serve the soup with small potatoes.

HOT CREAM SOUPS

Potato-Cucumber Soup

YIELD: 4 servings

Ingredients

12 oz fingerling potatoes, peeled and cut into chunks

¼ tsp salt for potato water

6 English cucumbers, peeled and cut into chunks

1 Tbsp fresh lime juice

1 oz garlic, diced

1 Tbsp lemon grass, chopped and loosely packed

½ cup Madeira wine

1 cup chicken stock (pg. 20)

½ cup heavy cream

1 cup crème fraîche (pg. 25)

¼ cup chives, chopped fine

½ tsp dill, chopped

½ tsp chervil, chopped

½ tsp mace

Dusting of lemon pepper

Procedure

In a saucepan, bring potato water to a boil. Add potatoes and salt. Boil them to just al dente—do not overcook them. Drain potatoes and dry them well. In a bowl, sprinkle cucumbers with the lime juice. Add potatoes, garlic, lemon grass, and Madeira and mix well. Place mixture in a food processor and puree to a fine consistency.

In a saucepan, combine chicken stock and cream and bring to a fast boil. Carefully add the puree to it and combine well. Reduce heat and gently simmer the soup for about 20 minutes, being careful not to burn it because of its thick consistency. At the last minute, whisk in the crème fraîche, chives, and seasonings. Check for correct seasoning and add a little more salt if needed. Serve the soup with a dollop of crème fraîche. This soup is also excellent when served ice cold!

NOTE: if regular cucumbers are used, all seeds need to be removed.

LEMON GRASS: a fairly new herb to western cuisine, and is an excellent addition to any dish that calls for a tangy taste.

Potato-Leek Soup

YIELD: 4 servings

Ingredients

½ lb Yukon gold potatoes,
  peeled and quartered

2 cups chicken stock, divided (pg. 20)

4 oz leeks (white parts only), diced

1 oz garlic, minced

¼ tsp mace, crumbled

1 tsp dill, chopped

1 Tbsp parsley, chopped

½ cup Madeira wine

1 cup heavy cream

½ cup crème fraîche (pg. 25)

¼ tsp lemon zest

Dusting of freshly ground white pepper

Procedure

Cover peeled potatoes with 1 cup of the chicken stock and boil until liquid is almost evaporated. DO NOT BURN POTATOES! Combine potatoes, leeks, garlic, mace, dill, and parsley in food processor and puree. In a saucepan, add the puree and mix with 1 cup chicken stock, Madeira, cream, and crème fraîche. Bring to a boil. Reduce heat and gently simmer the soup for about 15 minutes. Just before serving, stir in lemon zest and dust with white pepper. Garnish soup with seasoned croutons.

A word of caution: because of the thickness of the soup, it can easily burn. Whisk on occasion during cooking process.

Asparagus Soup

YIELD: 4 servings

Ingredients

8 oz green asparagus, cut,
  with tips set aside

½ cup chives, chopped

½ oz lemon grass, chopped

1 cup chicken stock (pg. 20)

½ cup cream sherry

1 cup heavy cream

½ cup crème fraîche (pg. 25)

½ cup asparagus tips

1 Tbsp chervil, chopped

Dusting of freshly ground pepper

Puff pastry leaves (pg. 64)

Procedure

In a saucepan combine cut asparagus, chives, lemon grass, and chicken stock. Bring to a boil and boil just until asparagus are tender. Puree in food processor. Combine with sherry, cream, and crème fraîche and bring back to a boil. Reduce the heat and gently simmer the soup for about 15 minutes, whisking it on occasion to keep it from burning. Just before serving, incorporate the asparagus tips. Season with the chopped chervil and pepper. Serve in soup bowls and garnish with baked puff pastry leaves.

Mushroom Soup

YIELD: 4 servings

Ingredients

12 oz shiitake mushrooms, sliced; divided

2 oz garlic, minced

¼ cup chives, chopped

1 Tbsp parsley, chopped

¼ cup olive oil, divided

½ cup sweet vermouth, divided

1 cup chicken stock (pg. 20)

1 cup heavy cream

½ cup crème fraîche (pg. 25)

1 Tbsp fresh thyme leaves

Dusting of freshly ground nutmeg and white pepper

Procedure

In a skillet, combine 8 ounces of sliced mushrooms with the garlic, chives, and parsley. Drizzle them with half of the olive oil and lightly sauté. Carefully deglaze with half the vermouth. Place mixture in a food processor and puree. In a saucepan combine the puree with the chicken stock, cream, and crème fraîche and bring to a boil. Reduce heat and gently simmer the soup for about 20 minutes. In a skillet, place the 4 ounces of mushrooms and season with the thyme leaves. Sprinkle with the rest of the olive oil and lightly sauté. Deglaze with the rest of the vermouth and add this to the rest of the soup. Finish off with a dusting of nutmeg and white pepper.

Zucchini-Squash Soup

YIELD: 4 servings

Ingredients

1 lb zucchinis, green, yellow, or mixed

2 oz leeks (white insides only), chopped

½ oz garlic, minced

1 tsp lemon grass, chopped

½ tsp salt

½ tsp lemon pepper (pg. 13)

2 cups chicken stock (pg. 20)

½ cup Madeira wine

½ cup heavy cream

½ cup crème fraîche (pg. 25)

Parmesan cheese, freshly grated

Procedure

Cut zucchinis into small chunks and place in saucepan. Add the leeks, garlic, lemon grass, salt, and pepper. Add the chicken stock and Madeira, and bring to a boil. Reduce heat and simmer just long enough to bring zucchinis to a tender stage. Puree in a food processor to a fine consistency. Return puree to saucepan and add the heavy cream and bring it back to a low boiling point, stirring at intervals so as not to burn the cream. Reduce the heat, whisk in the crème fraîche and gently simmer the soup for about 20 minutes. Just before serving, dust lightly with freshly grated parmesan cheese.

Artichoke Soup

YIELD: 4 servings

Ingredients

10 oz canned artichoke hearts, well drained

¼ cup shallots, chopped

½ cup chives, chopped

½ oz lemon grass, chopped

1 cup chicken stock (pg. 20)

½ cup Madeira wine

1 cup heavy cream

½ cup crème fraîche (pg. 25)

¼ cup parsley, chopped

1 tsp mace, finely ground

Puff pastry leaves (pg. 64)

Procedure

In a saucepan combine artichokes, shallots, chives, and lemon grass with chicken stock. Bring to a slow boil and then puree in a food processor. Return puree to saucepan and combine with Madeira, cream, and crème fraîche and bring to a boil. Reduce heat and gently simmer the soup for 15 minutes. Incorporate parsley and mace at the last minute. Serve the soup with baked puff pastry garnish.

Preparation with fresh artichokes

Use 12 baby artichokes with outer leaves, tops, and stems removed

2 small lemons

Pinch salt

2 garlic cloves, coarsely sliced

1 cup olive oil

Rub the baby artichokes vigorously with lemon and place in cold water. Add salt, lemon wedges, garlic, and olive oil to water and bring to a boil. Boil until the artichokes reach the "falling apart" stage. Remove the artichokes from the water and pass them through a food mill fitted with a coarse blade, getting as much of the artichokes as possible through the mill. Remove all fibrous and coarse matter. Proceed with above preparation.

Butternut Squash Soup

YIELD: 4 servings

Ingredients

1 small butternut squash, about 1 lb

3 oz fresh ginger, grated

1 Tbsp garlic, minced

2 oz chives, chopped

4–5 sprigs parsley, chopped

1 oz lemon extract

½ tsp salt

½ tsp lemon pepper (pg. 13)

½ cup Madeira wine

1 cup chicken stock (pg. 20)

1 cup heavy cream

½ cup yogurt

Dusting of nutmeg

Procedure

Cut squash lengthwise in half and remove the seeds. Place in a shallow baking dish, meat side up, lightly sprinkle with salt, and add enough water in the pan to prevent burning the squash during poaching procedure. Cover dish with aluminum foil and poach in preheated oven at 450 degrees for about 1 hour. Squash should be soft but not mushy to the touch.

Scoop out the meat and combine with the ginger, garlic, chives, and parsley. Add the lemon extract, salt, and pepper. Add the Madeira and puree the mixture in a food processor to a fine consistency. Place the puree in a stock pot, add the chicken stock and cream and bring to a boil. Since the puree burns easily, it needs to be stirred frequently at intervals until boiling point. Reduce heat and gently simmer the soup for about 20 minutes. Whisk in the yogurt and just before serving dust with freshly grated nutmeg. Check for correct seasoning and add more salt if needed.

Pumpkin Soup
Acorn Squash Soup

Proceed as for Butternut Squash Soup above, substituting one pound of alternate squash.

Carrot-Tomato Soup

YIELD: 4 servings

Ingredients

4 oz carrots, grated

2 oz green onions, chopped

6 oz tomatoes, chopped

1 oz garlic, minced

½ cup tomato juice

½ cup cream sherry

1 cup chicken stock (pg. 20)

1 cup heavy cream

½ cup crème fraîche (pg. 25)

1 Tbsp chervil, chopped

¼ tsp dill

Dusting of freshly ground white pepper

Procedure

In a saucepan combine the grated carrots, green onions, tomatoes, and garlic. Add tomato juice and sherry and gently boil until carrots are just tender. Place in a food processor and puree. Return to saucepan and combine with the chicken stock, cream, and crème fraîche. Bring to a boil, reduce heat and simmer for about 20 minutes. Stir in chervil and dill just before serving. Dust with ground white pepper. Serve with parmesan-lemon shortbread (page 67).

Artichoke Soup

FAWN BROOK FAMILY MEMORIES

Cravings

Adrieke: When Chris and I lived in Ft. Worth, Texas, one of the cravings I had was for my dad's Carrot-Tomato Cream Soup. Although I'm sure Chris would have driven clear to Allenspark at two in the morning to get me a bowl of soup, I doubt he would have been too happy about doing so. That year I'll never forget the euphoria, not to mention the look of relief on my husband's face, when the mail came for my birthday. In the box was the recipe. It still holds a position of honor in my collection of cookbooks.

Kara: I crave Hermann's fabulous soups! They are wonderful and taste delicious in every season of life.

COLD CREAM SOUPS

Basic Stock for Cold Fruit Soups

YIELD: 1 cup

Ingredients

¼ cup chicken stock (pg. 20)

2 cups dry Riesling wine

¼ cup pure maple syrup

1 cinnamon stick, about 3 inches long,
   broken into small pieces

1 bay leaf, crumbled

½ tsp lemon grass, chopped

1 vanilla bean, very finely chopped

Combine and crush in a mortar:

4 whole allspice berries

4 white pepper corns

3 cloves

2 star anise

Procedure

In a saucepan combine the chicken stock, wine, maple syrup, and all spices and herbs, including chopped vanilla bean. Bring to a boil, then reduce the heat and gently simmer until liquid is reduced to about 1 cup. Strain the stock with a fine wire-mesh sieve and use when called for in the following recipes.

Peach-Raspberry Soup

YIELD: 4 servings

Ingredients

16 oz ripe peaches (approximately 4 fruits depending on size)

1 Tbsp fresh lime juice

1 cup fruit stock (above)

⅓ cup peach nectar or peach liqueur

1 cup heavy cream

½ cup crème fraîche (pg. 25)

Fresh raspberries, approximately 8 berries per serving

Fresh mint leaves for garnish

Procedure

Quarter and de-stone peaches and place in a saucepan. Add the lime juice, stock, liqueur, and cream and bring to a boil. Reduce heat and gently simmer until the fruit reaches a soft, tender stage. *Do not overcook.* Puree in a food processor. Whisk in the crème fraîche and refrigerate until cold. Just before serving, stir in the fresh berries. Garnish the soup with a thinly sliced peach fan and fresh mint leaves.

Apricot-Blackberry Soup

Proceed as for Peach-Raspberry Soup above, but substitute apricots, blackberries, and apricot liqueur.

Cherry-Ginger Soup

YIELD: 4 servings

Ingredients

1 cup fruit stock (pg. 60)

1 cup heavy cream

1 Tbsp lime juice

1 Tbsp rose water

⅓ cup cherry liqueur

1 lb pitted dark cherries, plus 12 lightly poached cherries

½ cup crème fraîche (pg. 25)

4 oz fresh ginger, peeled and finely chopped

Fresh mint leaves for garnish

Procedure

In a saucepan combine stock, cream, lime juice, rose water, and liqueur. Add 1 pound cherries and bring to boil. Reduce heat and simmer cherries to a tender stage. Remove all cherries from liquid. Very gently poach the 12 cherries for garnish and set aside. Puree the first batch of cherries in a food processor. Place puree in a bowl and add the liquid back in. Whisk in crème fraîche and ginger, and place in refrigerator to cool. Garnish the soup with the poached cherries and mint leaves.

Rhubarb-Strawberry Soup

YIELD: 4 servings

Ingredients

1 cup fruit stock (pg. 60)

1 Tbsp rose water

1 Tbsp fresh lime juice

⅓ cup strawberry liqueur

1 cup heavy cream

16 oz fresh rhubarb, peeled and chopped into 1-inch long chunks

½ cup crème fraîche (pg. 25)

16 oz fresh strawberries, sliced

Fresh mint leaf for garnish

Procedure

In a saucepan combine stock, rose water, lime juice, liqueur, and cream. Add the rhubarb and bring to a boil. Reduce the heat and simmer until rhubarb is tender. *Do not overcook.* Puree in a food processor. Whisk in the crème fraîche, add the sliced strawberries and refrigerate until cold. Garnish the soup with a strawberry fan and a fresh mint leaf.

To preserve fresh ginger, peel off the rind, dice the root, and preserve in dry sherry. The sherry is also good to drink afterward!

Apple-Blueberry Soup

YIELD: 4 servings

Ingredients

16 oz tart, firm apples (approximately 4)
cored and quartered, do not peel
1 Tbsp fresh lime juice
1 cup fruit stock (pg. 60)
⅓ cup Calvados brandy
1 cup heavy cream
½ cup crème fraîche (pg. 25)
1 cup fresh blueberries, firmly packed
Fresh mint sprig for garnish

Procedure

Place the cored and quartered apples in a saucepan and sprinkle with lime juice to prevent discoloring. Add the stock, Calvados, and cream. Bring to a boil. Reduce heat and gently simmer until the fruit reaches a soft, tender stage. *Do not overcook.* Puree in food processor. Whisk in the crème fraîche and refrigerate until cold. Just before serving, fold in the berries. Garnish with fresh apple slices and a sprig of fresh mint.

Asian Pear–Cranberry Soup

Proceed as for Apple-Blueberry Soup above. Poach 1 cup of fresh cranberries lightly in cranberry juice, fortified with a cup of Port, with enough liquid to just cover the berries. Substitute 16 oz. Asian pears for the apples. Use pear brandy or liqueur instead of Calvados.

One of the many community lunches.

Garnishes
for Hot Soups

Toasted Croutons

Slice a French baguette into ¼-inch slices. Lightly drizzle with olive oil and season with coarse sea salt and thyme leaves. Very lightly toast in hot oven.

Puff Pastry

This is fun to make if you have time, but it may also be purchased.

YIELD: 11 oz

Ingredients

4 oz sifted all-purpose white flour, plus about
    1 oz for dusting
2 oz softened unsalted butter
3 oz ice cold water
¼ tsp fine sea salt

To obtain good results in making Puff Pastry, remember the following:
  A. Butter should be soft, but not too soft. It should bend easily, but not break.
  B. Water must be ice cold.
  C. The folding, turning, and resting times between work procedures are critical.

Procedure

Place flour into a shallow bowl. Make a well in the center and slowly add the water. Quickly incorporate water with the tips of your fingers in the flour, then add the salt, working the dough continuously until it forms a smooth ball. Make an incision cross-wise, wrap in plastic wrap, and refrigerate for 15 minutes.

Place dough on a floured surface and with the palms of your hands punch dough out to an even-size square, about 7 x 7 inches. Brushing off any excess flour, form butter into an even-size square, about ¾-inch thick, and place it in the center of the dough. Fold each side of the dough over the butter,

forming an envelope, being sure seams overlap each other on top. Dust with flour and turn envelope seam-side down. Carefully and lightly roll the dough out to a rectangle, about 12 x 8 inches, being sure that no butter inside the dough escapes through the seams. Brush off any excess flour and fold long ends of dough towards the center; the two ends should meet, but not overlap. Then fold right side over left side and again roll out to a rectangle of 12 x 8 inches. Again fold long ends toward the center, fold right side over left side, re-wrap and refrigerate for 15 minutes.

Again, roll out to a rectangle, fold long ends to the center, then fold right side over left side, re-wrap and refrigerate for 15 minutes *Repeat procedure 3 more times.* Wrap the finished product and refrigerate for up to 12 hours before using it.

Baked Puff Pastry Leaves "Fleurons"

YIELD: 10 leaves

Ingredients

6 oz puff pastry (left)
Egg wash (pg. 3)
Dusting of salt
Dusting of freshly grated parmesan cheese

Procedure

Lightly dust countertop with flour. Place puff pastry in the center and roll out to a rectangle, about 9 x 7 inches, and ⅛-inch thick. Cut out 10 leaves with a leaf-shaped cookie cutter and place them on a cookie sheet sprayed with cooking spray. With a small knife cut incisions in a vein pattern into the leaves. Brush lightly with egg wash, dust with parmesan and salt and bake in a preheated oven at 500 degrees for 8 minutes. Reverse cookie sheet and bake another 2 or 3 minutes or until fleurons are lightly golden brown. Serve with your choice of cream soup.

Rolled Pheasant Pastry

YIELD: approximately 6 servings

Ingredients

4 oz puff pastry at room temperature (pg. 64)
6 oz boneless skinless pheasant breasts
2 oz duck or goose liver
1 whole egg, well beaten
Dusting of freshly grated nutmeg
½ tsp salt
Dusting of freshly ground white pepper
1 tsp each of chopped parsley, chives, and
     thyme
1 medium garlic clove, finely diced
1 egg yolk, well beaten

Procedure

Lightly dust a strong linen cloth (20 x 24 inches) with flour. Place puff pastry on it and roll out to a rectangle, approximately 6 x 8 inches. Cube the meat and liver and place it in a food processor. Add the beaten whole egg, nutmeg, salt, and pepper, and process until a fine mousse-like consistency is achieved. Place the mousse into a bowl and add all the chopped herbs and seasonings. Combine mixture well and with a wet spatula spread the mousse mixture evenly over the puff pastry, being sure that the mixture is spread to the ends of the dough.

With both hands, take hold at the ends of the cloth. Gently lift it and very tightly roll strudel away from you, being sure seam of strudel ends up at the bottom. Double line a metal sheet pan with parchment paper, spray with cooking spray, and place the strudel onto it, being sure that the seam is on the bottom of the pan. Tuck in the ends and seal them off. With a skewer prick the top of the strudel in several places for steam to escape during baking procedure. Brush the strudel with the beaten egg yolk and bake in a preheated oven at 425 degrees for 25 minutes. Reverse the pan and bake for another 10 minutes. The strudel should be nicely golden brown on top and sides. Slice into even-sized serving pieces and serve hot with chicken, beef, or game broth.

Spatzle (Deep Fried)

YIELD: 4 servings

Ingredients

¼ cup all-purpose white flour
2 large eggs
1 Tbsp lavender flowers
Pinch of salt
Dusting of nutmeg
Dusting of white pepper
~2½ cups canola or peanut oil

Procedure

Combine all ingredients except oil and mix well to form a runny batter. Heat oil to 350 degrees in a pan with a heavy bottom. With a small spoon, drop dollops of batter (about the size of a quarter) into the hot oil and fry until golden brown. Remove spatzles and drain on paper towels. Serve as garnish with clear beef or chicken broth, or sprinkle the spatzles with cinnamon and sugar and serve with Vanilla Sauce (page 148) as a light dessert.

Kajetan and wife Kara.

Baked Cheese Puffs

YIELD: 12 puffs

Ingredients

4½ oz water
2 oz unsalted butter
¼ tsp salt
2½ oz all-purpose white flour
4 oz plain goat cheese at room temperature
Dusting of cayenne pepper
1/4 tsp mace
2 large eggs

Procedure

Place water, butter, and salt in a saucepan and bring to a boil. As soon as butter is melted, add flour at once and mix quickly with a wooden spoon. Reduce heat and stir in the cheese and add the cayenne and mace. Turn off the heat and beat in the eggs, one at a time. The dough should easily pull away from the sides of the pan and should be smooth and shiny looking. Line a baking sheet with double parchment paper. Fit a pastry bag with a medium size star tip and fill with the dough. Pipe out 12 even-sized stars and bake in a preheated oven at 375 degrees for 45 minutes. Rotate the tray and bake for another 15 minutes. The puffs should be golden brown. Serve with clear broth, or chicken or beef soup.

Pancake Egg Noodles (Classic French Crêpes)

YIELD: 10 crêpes

Ingredients

3 whole large eggs
Pinch of salt
1 oz butter, melted and cooled
2¼ cups whole milk
4 oz sifted all-purpose white flour
Dusting of freshly grated nutmeg
Pinch of lemon pepper (pg. 13)
Grape seed oil to brush crêpe pans

Procedure

In a mixing bowl combine the eggs, salt, and melted/cooled butter and whisk until a thick fluffy consistency is achieved. Slowly add the milk, reduce speed and slowly incorporate the flour, nutmeg, and lemon pepper. Mix the batter well, being sure no lumps of flour remain. Brush crêpe pans (or skillet) with oil and set over high heat. As soon as pans are sizzling hot, add a small amount of batter, about 3½ ounces. Nicely brown one side, flip, and brown the other side. Adjust heat as needed and add more oil to the pans as needed. Place browned crêpes on parchment paper to cool. Roll up cooled crêpes and slice to desired thickness. Serve as garnish with hot consommé or broth.

Parmesan-Lemon Shortbread

YIELD: 10 servings, 2 per serving

Ingredients

½ cup all-purpose white flour
½ Tbsp baking powder
Pinch chopped parsley
Pinch lemon pepper (pg. 13)
Pinch sea salt
Dusting of freshly grated nutmeg
2 oz unsalted butter, softened
1 large egg yolk
2 oz grated parmesan cheese
1 tsp lemon zest
½ cup heavy cream
Egg wash (pg. 3)

Procedure

In a bowl combine flour, baking powder, parsley, pepper, salt, and nutmeg. Mix well and work in the softened butter, a little at a time. Add the egg yolk, grated parmesan, and lemon zest and combine well. Add the cream and mix until a smooth dough is achieved. Form a ball, wrap it in plastic wrap and let it rest in a cool place for 2 hours.

Form 1-ounce balls and roll them out on a flat surface to about 1½-inch long sticks. Place them on a cookie sheet, spaced ½-inch apart. With a sharp knife, make a few slight incisions on each one. Brush them with egg wash and bake in a preheated oven at 375 degrees for about 25 minutes or until lightly golden brown. Serve with hot cream soups.

Spinach-Cheese Gnocchies

YIELD: 22 1-oz dumplings

Ingredients

2 oz cubed white bread, crust removed
1 oz butter
10 oz peeled potatoes, Yukon Gold
    or fingerlings
4 oz plain goat cheese
1 oz baby spinach, chopped fine
2 large egg yolks
1 large whole egg
½ cup all-purpose white flour,
    plus a dusting if needed
Dusting of freshly grated nutmeg
1 tsp salt
1 tsp lemon pepper (pg. 13)
~4 cups chicken stock

Procedure

In a skillet lightly toast the cubed bread in butter. Parboil whole peeled potatoes in lightly salted water. *Do not cook them all the way!* Drain water and dry potatoes well. Cut potatoes into small cubes. In a mixing bowl combine potatoes, bread, cheese, spinach, egg yolks, egg, flour, nutmeg, salt, and pepper. Mix well until a smooth dough is achieved. Remove dough from bowl and dust it with flour. Place on a tray, cover with a warm cloth and let it rest in a draught-free place for about 2 hours.

Dust hands generously with flour and form small 1-ounce dumplings. Bring chicken stock to a boil and gently drop dumplings into boiling stock, one at a time. Reduce heat and gently simmer them until done, about 10 minutes. They should rise to the surface when done. Check with a toothpick for doneness; toothpick needs to come out clean. Remove dumplings from stock. Serve dumplings plain as garnish for chicken consommé or any other broth, or lightly fry them in hot butter and generously dust them with grated parmesan cheese.

FAWN BROOK FAMILY MEMORIES

Grandkids

Our son Alex and I had the privilege of living with my parents during one of my husband Chris' deployments. For those reading this who have children, I'm sure you can relate to the changes that come over parents when they become grand-parents. Growing up, my brother and I knew exactly what we could and couldn't get away with in our dad's kitchen. Going behind the counter with him was sign-ing your death warrant, sneaking food out of the pantry was grounds for dis-ownment. However, as a grandchild you apparently have carte blanche in Opa's kitchen. Alex was about eighteen months old and he had both Opa and Oma wrapped around more than one finger. As any responsible mother, I laid down the ground rules to my parents: not too much sugar, don't let him play with knives ... they may have listened to the knife rule, but the sugar? Not only did my son get a candied ginger addiction, he found it was okay with Opa to dance, run, and jump in the kitchen AND to help himself to the counters full of food. His favorite bins were the endless sup-ply of raisins, ginger, and, oddly enough, peppercorns. I tried to take advantage of Alex's freedom in the kitchen and needless to say, I didn't get away with it.

Duck Meat Quenelles

YIELD: approximately 14 2-oz dumplings

Ingredients

1 large egg
¼ cup heavy cream
2 oz white bread, crust removed and cubed
6 oz duck meat, cubed
¼ tsp salt
Dusting of white pepper
½ tsp mace
¼ cup bread crumbs
½ tsp thyme leaves
½ Tbsp parsley, finely chopped
1 Tbsp chives, chopped
1 medium garlic clove, finely minced
~4 cups chicken stock

Procedure

In a bowl whisk the egg with the cream and com-bine with the cubed bread. Season cubed duck meat with salt, pepper, and mace. Mix with the bread, add bread crumbs and puree the mixture in a food processor to a medium-coarse consistency. Add all chopped and minced herbs and combine well. Bring chicken stock to a boil. With a soup spoon, form small 1-ounce oblong dumplings. Carefully drop them into the boiling stock, one at a time. Reduce heat and gently sim-mer them for about 10 minutes. They should be done as they float to the surface of the simmering stock. Serve with your choice of a clear soup.

Alex in Opa's kitchen.

Side Dishes

Mixed Salad

YIELD: 4 servings

Salad consists of vegetable mold in aspic, marinated mushrooms, cauliflower, English cucumbers, juliennes of roasted red peppers (recipes follow), and butter lettuce. To serve the salad, place butter lettuce on a plate and center the aspic on top. Surround the aspic with vegetables, garnish with roasted pine nuts, and serve with toasted Roquefort points. Salad may also be served without the aspic.

Marinated Mushrooms
Ingredients

8 small button mushrooms or 4 large ones, split into quarters

1 Tbsp lemon juice

Pinch of sea salt

3 garlic cloves, smashed

1 sprig fresh rosemary

½ cup extra virgin olive oil

Procedure

Place mushrooms in a skillet. Sprinkle lemon juice and all seasonings over them. Add the olive oil and bring it to a full boil. Reduce the heat and simmer until mushrooms are soft to the touch. Refrigerate mushrooms with all the juices overnight.

Marinated Cauliflower
Ingredients

4 medium-size rosettes of cauliflower

Dash of sea salt

3 plump whole cloves

1 cup chardonnay wine

¼ cup olive oil

Procedure

Combine everything in a skillet and bring to a boil. Reduce heat and simmer for about 4 minutes. Refrigerate the cauliflower in the liquid overnight.

Marinated English Cucumbers
Ingredients

    8-inch long cucumber, sliced into ½-inch thick strips

    ½ Tbsp sea salt

    1 tsp dill, chopped

    1 Tbsp lime juice

    ½ cup extra virgin olive oil

    1 Tbsp Reggiano parmesan cheese, freshly grated

Procedure

Place cucumber strips in a bowl and dust with salt and dill. Add the lime juice and olive oil and sprinkle grated cheese over the top. Refrigerate overnight.

Juliennes of Roasted Red Peppers
Ingredients

    ¼ cup extra virgin olive oil

    1 oz shallots, sliced to fine discs

    4 oz red peppers, deseeded and julienned to ½-inch thick strips

    Dusting of sea salt

    2 Tbsp fresh orange juice

Procedure

In a skillet bring olive oil to bubbling point. Add the shallots and lightly glaze them transparent. Add the pepper strips. Season with a dusting of salt and just lightly sauté the peppers. Pour the orange juice over them. Remove from the heat and refrigerate overnight.

A good time at a community lunch.

Vegetable Mold in Aspic

Ingredients

2 2-inch round PVC pipes, cut 1½ inches long

2 oz hearts of palm, cut 1½ inches long

½ oz baby red pepper pod, seeds removed,
   cut into 4 equal strips and lightly roasted in grape seed oil

8 equal-size 1½-inch long baby carrots, lightly steamed

4 artichoke bottom halves, steamed "al dente"

4 sundried tomatoes, marinated in oil, well drained

4 equal-sized ribs of celery hearts

1 cup sparkling white wine

1 Tbsp lime juice

Dash of salt

1 Tbsp plain gelatin

Sprigs of parsley

Procedure

Coat the inside of the PVC pipes with cooking spray and place them on a flat tray. Arrange all vegetables standing up in a nice pattern in the mold. In a skillet, combine sparkling wine, lime juice, and salt. Bring to a boil. Reduce heat to simmer and quickly dissolve gelatin in it. With a spoon, ladle a spoonful of the liquid over the vegetable molds. Refrigerate the molds until well set, about 30 minutes. Bring the liquid back to simmer and ladle another spoonful over the molds. Again refrigerate until aspic is well set. Repeat procedure one more time. The molds should be nicely covered with the aspic. Refrigerate overnight. Dip the molds out of the PVC pipe and with a wet, hot knife cut the molds into 2 discs. Garnish them with a sprig of parsley.

NOTE: This procedure must be done with a bottomless vessel or it is impossible to get the aspic out. I have found nothing that works better than PVC pipe.

Warm Potato Salad

YIELD: 4 servings

Ingredients

1 lb potatoes, Yukon gold are preferred

2 oz lean bacon, chopped

¼ cup grape seed oil

1 oz shallots, finely diced

½ oz elephant garlic, finely minced

1 Tbsp chives, chopped

1 tsp parsley, chopped

¼ cup scented vinegar (pg. 32)

1 Tbsp white wine vinegar

¼ tsp sea salt

¼ tsp lemon pepper (pg. 13)

¼ tsp thyme leaves

Procedure

Boil whole potatoes in lightly salted water until soft and done to the touch. Drain off all water. Peel them as soon as they can be handled, then slice them. Place potatoes in a bowl and set aside. In a skillet, brown bacon until crisp. Add the oil. Reduce the heat and add the shallots, garlic, chives, and parsley, and lightly sauté. Add the vinegars and simmer for a few minutes. Season the potatoes with the salt, pepper, and thyme leaves. Pour the simmering dressing over the potatoes and mix well.

Adrieke and dad on graduation night

NOTE: To cook potatoes, pastas, noodles, dumplings, etc., always boil the water first. Season with salt after items are immersed in water. Boil potatoes or any root vegetables, but simmer pastas, noodles, or dumplings until they are done. Drain off all water immediately after items are done. Let potatoes or dumplings drain in a wire-mesh sieve. Pastas and noodles need to be rinsed in cold water right after cooking procedure and then left to dry in a wire-mesh sieve or colander.

Potato Pancakes

YIELD: 4 servings

Ingredients

1 Yukon gold potato, approximately 10 oz

Lightly salted cold water

Few drops of lemon juice

1 Tbsp chives, chopped

1 Tbsp parsley, chopped

½ oz garlic, finely minced

½ oz shallots, thinly sliced

¼ tsp sea salt

¼ tsp freshly ground white pepper

Pinch of mace

1 large egg, plus 1 large egg yolk

1 Tbsp olive oil

1 Tbsp all-purpose white flour

2 Tbsp grape seed oil

Procedure

Wash potato, peel and slice into juliennes. Plunge immediately into cold, salted water. Squeeze in a few drops of lemon juice to prevent potatoes from discoloring. Drain them of all liquid and pat them dry on paper towels. Place dry potatoes in a bowl and add chives, parsley, garlic, shallots, salt, pepper, and mace; combine well. Whisk in the eggs and olive oil. Mix in flour, a dusting at a time, being sure no lumps of flour remain. Divide mixture into four equal parts and flatten into pancakes. Place grape seed oil in frying skillet and set over high heat. As soon as skillet and oil are hot, carefully place individual pancakes in skillet and brown them on both sides to crisp.

Potato Dumplings

YIELD: 4 servings

Ingredients

6 oz Yukon gold or white potatoes peeled and grated

½ oz butter

1 Tbsp olive oil

1 oz white bread, cubed

1 Tbsp chives chopped

1 Tbsp parsley chopped

½ oz shallots, minced

¼ tsp sea salt

¼ tsp lemon pepper

Dusting of nutmeg

1 large whole egg

1 large egg yolk

1 cup all purpose white flour

Procedure

Grate the potatoes and plunge them right away into lightly salted cold water. Drain and pat dry with paper towels, making sure all moisture is removed from them. Place potatoes in a bowl. In a skillet, lightly brown the cubed bread with the butter and olive oil. Add the chives, parsley, and shallots. Mix well. Drain off all grease, then add mixture to the potatoes. Season with salt, pepper, and nutmeg. Add the egg and egg yolk and incorporate well. Slowly mix in the flour until an elastic dough is achieved. Add more flour if needed. With well-floured hands, form 6 to 8 round even-sized dumplings. Bring lightly salted water to a boil and gently immerse the dumplings, one at a time. Bring water back to a boil, reduce the heat and gently simmer for about 15 to 20 minutes. Dumplings will rise to the surface when done. If needed, carefully loosen them from the bottom with a kitchen spoon.

Baked Potato Puffs

YIELD: 6 puffs

Ingredients

1 lb potatoes, fingerling or Yukon gold are preferred

Dash of sea salt

Pâte à Chou, consisting of:

    2 oz sifted all purpose white flour

    1 oz grated Swiss gruyere cheese

    Dusting of fresh grated nutmeg

    Dash cayenne pepper

    4 oz water

    1 oz butter

    1 large egg

Procedure

Bring a pot of water to boil and add whole potatoes. As soon as water boils again, season with a pinch of salt. Boil potatoes al dente. *Do not overcook them!* Drain off all water and pat them dry. Peel them as soon as they can be handled. Mash them right away to a fine consistency and set aside.

FOR THE PÂTÉ À CHOUX, in a bowl mix the flour with the cheese, nutmeg, and cayenne pepper; set aside. In a saucepan combine the 4 ounces of water and the butter and bring to a fast boil. As soon as the water boils and the butter is melted, immerse flour/cheese mixture all at once into the boiling water. With a wooden spoon, mix as fast as possible. Remove from heat and beat in the egg. The mixture should be smooth and glossy.

Remove the mixture from pan and combine right away with the mashed potatoes. Spray a sheet pan with cooking spray. Fit a pastry bag with a large star tip, fill it with the potato mixture and pipe out 6 even-sized star puffs. Bake in a pre-heated oven at 375 degrees for 45 minutes. Rotate the tray and bake for another 15 minutes. Potato puffs should be nicely golden brown.

Baked Soufflé Potatoes

Baked Soufflé Potatoes

YIELD: 4 servings

Ingredients

½ lb potatoes, Yukon gold
   or fingerlings

1 oz butter at room temperature

¼ cup heavy cream

½ lb tart firm apples, cored,
   Granny Smith or Winesap

Dash of fresh lime juice

1 large whole egg

1 large egg yolk

1 tsp parsley, chopped

1 Tbsp chives, chopped

1 tsp garlic, finely minced

½ tsp sea salt

¼ tsp mace

Dusting of lemon pepper (pg. 13)

Few drops of garlic oil to
   brush soufflé dish

Dusting of fine bread crumbs

Procedure

Bring a pot of water to boiling point. Add whole potatoes and a pinch of salt. Boil potatoes until they are soft. Drain all water and dry them on paper towels. Peel them as soon as they can be handled. Place them in a bowl and mash them to a coarse consistency. Mix in the butter and cream. Grate the apples and sprinkle with lime juice to prevent discoloring. Drain apples of all moisture and mix them with the potatoes. Whisk together the egg and egg yolk and mix them with the potato/apple mixture. Mix in all seasonings and herbs. Brush soufflé dish with garlic oil and place potato/apple mixture into the dish. Dust generously with fine bread crumbs and bake the dish in a preheated oven at 375 degrees for 30 minutes, or until sides of the dish are bubbling and top is nicely browned.

Potato Croquets

YIELD: 8 2½ oz croquets (about 3 inches)

Ingredients

½ lb potatoes, peeled

½ cup almonds,
   toasted and ground

1 large egg yolk

Sea salt and pepper to taste

Dusting of nutmeg

Pâte à Chou, consisting of:

   2 oz butter at room temperature

   2 oz all-purpose white flour

   1 large egg

   ¼ cup potato flour

   ½ cup breadcrumbs

Deep fat frying oil at 350 degrees

Procedure

Bring a pot of water to boiling point, add peeled potatoes and lightly boil al dente. Drain all water and dry potatoes on paper towels. Let potatoes cool, then grate them. In a bowl, combine ingredients for Pâte à Chou and set aside.

Combine grated potatoes with almonds, egg yolk, salt, pepper, and nutmeg. Add the pâte à chou. Thicken mixture with potato flour until a smooth dough is achieved. Dough should be elastic and not sticky. With the palm of your hands, roll the dough out into a rope and slice into equal pieces. Roll them through the breadcrumbs and fry them to a nice golden color.

Yorkshire Pudding

YIELD: approximately 6 servings

Ingredients

3 large whole eggs

1 cup whole milk

2 oz butter, melted

1 tsp sea salt

1 cup all-purpose white flour

Grape seed oil to brush
 pudding molds

Procedure

In a bowl combine eggs, milk, and melted butter and whisk until foamy. In a separate bowl mix the salt into the flour, then whisk into egg batter. Mix until a smooth batter, free of any lumps, is achieved. Ladle batter into well-oiled pudding molds to about ¾ full. Place molds on a sheet pan and bake in a preheated oven at 375 degrees for about 45 minutes or until tops are golden brown. Remove from oven and place on a cooling rack. Gently remove the baked puddings as soon as the molds can be handled. Keep them warm until ready to use.

NOTE: If crispier and drier pudding is desired, when the pudding is done baking, make an incision on top of pudding with a sharp knife, turn off the heat and keep them in the oven for another 15 minutes. Serve the pudding with plenty of gravy or roasting juices.

Bread Pudding

YIELD: 4 servings

Ingredients

5 oz French baguette

5 oz butter

½ Tbsp vanilla sugar (pg. 150)

Zest of ½ small lemon

4 oz sun-dried cherries

½ cup pure maple syrup

2 large eggs

½ cup heavy cream

Procedure

Slice bread about 1½-inches thick. Generously spread each side with butter and place into a 1½-inch-deep baking dish. Sprinkle sugar and lemon zest over them. In a saucepan, combine cherries and maple syrup, and poach over medium heat until they are soft; pour over the bread. Whisk together the eggs and cream. Pour over the bread/cherry mixture and let stand for about 30 to 40 minutes.

Place in a preheated oven at 375 degrees and bake for about 30 minutes, or until top is nicely browned. Serve as a side dish with roasted duck and other fowl, or as dessert. If served as dessert, dust with powdered sugar and cinnamon and serve with vanilla sauce (page 148) and whipped cream.

Bread-Bacon Dumplings

YIELD: 4 servings

Ingredients

2 oz butter

2 oz smoked lean bacon, diced

1½ oz stale white bread, cut into small croutons

1 Tbsp chives, chopped

1 Tbsp parsley, chopped

½ tsp salt

1 large whole egg

1 large egg yolk

⅓ cup whole milk

Dusting of nutmeg

Dusting of white pepper

1½ cups all-purpose white flour

Procedure

In a skillet bring the butter to a melting point. Add the bacon and fry until crisp. Add the croutons and nicely toast them on all sides. Add the chives, parsley, and salt; remove from heat. In a bowl, whisk the egg and egg yolk until fluffy. Mix in the milk, nutmeg, and pepper. Add the bread/bacon mixture and with a wooden spoon, mix in the flour a little at a time. Work it until an elastic dough is achieved. Add flour as needed until dough loosens easily from the sides of the bowl. Cover the bowl with a warm kitchen towel and let it rest for about 30 minutes.

Bring a pot of water to a boiling point and lightly season with salt. Form 4 even-sized dumplings and drop them one by one into the boiling water. Loosen the dumplings from the bottom of the pot with a kitchen spoon should they stick to it. Dumplings will rise to the surface when done. Simmer them for another 5 to 8 minutes. Insert a wooden toothpick or skewer. If the toothpick comes out clean, the dumplings will be done. Remove them from the water immediately.

Saffron Egg Noodles

YIELD: 4 servings

Ingredients

1 cup sifted all-pupose white flour

1 tsp sea salt

Pinch of saffron

Dusting of nutmeg

1 tsp chives, finely chopped

1 large whole egg

1 egg yolk

1 Tbsp cold water

1 tsp extra virgin olive oil

Some melted butter, just enough to heat noodles as stated in the recipe

Dusting of parmesan cheese

Procedure

Place flour in a bowl and make a well in the center. Add the seasonings and the egg and egg yolk to it and with the tips of your fingers incorporate everything with the flour. Slowly mix in the cold water and the oil and work it until a smooth elastic dough is achieved. If the dough seems too dry, add a few more drops of olive oil. Cover dough with a warm kitchen towel and let it rest for 30 minutes.

Place the dough on a lightly floured board and roll the dough out to a rectangle, about 10 x 12 inches. Lightly dust the dough with flour and gently roll it up. With a sharp knife cut dough to noodle-size strips, about ½-inch wide. Place the strips, unrolled, on a tray lined with parchment paper and let the noodles dry for about 30 minutes.

In a pot bring lightly salted water to a boil and drop the noodles a few at a time into the water, keeping them separated with a fork. Reduce the heat and gently simmer noodles for about 5 to 8 minutes. Check for doneness; drain into a wire-mesh sieve and immediately rinse them in cold water. Before serving, lightly heat noodles in melted butter in a skillet and dust them with parmesan cheese as they are served.

Saffron
There is absolutely no substitute for the taste, texture, and color of this most precious of all spices.

Bamboo Rice with Crystallized Ginger

YIELD: 4 servings

Ingredients

4 Tbsp black truffle oil

1 cup onions, finely diced

½ cup bamboo rice

½ cup basmati rice

2 cups chicken broth (pg. 20)

¼ cup crystallized ginger

Procedure

In a deep skillet heat the oil, add the onions and glaze them. Stir in the bamboo and basmati rice and coat the rice well with the hot oil. Reduce the heat and carefully pour in the chicken broth. Bring to a fast boil, reduce the heat, and cover the skillet with a lid or aluminum foil. Gently simmer the rice for about 20 minutes, and then check for doneness. Simmer the rice longer if needed and at the last minute stir in the ginger.

Sauerkraut

YIELD: 4 servings

Ingredients

4 oz cored apple chunks

Sprinkle of lemon juice

1 lb well-drained fresh sauerkraut

¼ cup grape seed oil

3 oz bacon, finely diced

½ oz garlic, finely minced

4 oz onions, diced

1½ cups dry Riesling wine

1 tsp salt

1 bay leaf

¼ cup caraway seeds

Dusting of white pepper

Procedure

Sprinkle apple chunks with lemon juice, combine with drained sauerkraut and set aside. In a saucepan, combine grape seed oil and bacon and over high heat crisp the bacon. Add garlic and just lightly brown. Add the onions and sweat them. Add the sauerkraut with the apples and mix well with bacon mixture. Add the Riesling and all seasonings. Stir it well and bring to boiling point. Reduce heat and gently simmer the sauerkraut until apples are nice and tender, but not mushy. Stir occasionally to prevent the sauerkraut from burning.

A word of caution: When purchasing sauerkraut, buy only from reliable sources. By all means avoid canned products. If the sauerkraut is not under proper refrigeration, do NOT use it.

Did you know? Sauerkraut is not an invention of the Germans, Austrians, Alsatians, or Swiss. It was eaten by Chinese laborers building the Great Wall over 2000 years ago. It has been recorded that it built up their stamina and strength. It is an excellent source of vitamins C and B, and its fresh juices prevent fat build up in your body so it will help in reducing cholesterol.

Braised Red Cabbage

YIELD: 4 servings

Ingredients

12 oz cleaned and cored red cabbage

4 oz apples, firm and tart, cored

⅓ cup lemon juice

¼ cup grape seed oil

3 oz bacon, finely diced

1 oz garlic, finely minced

4 oz onions, diced

¼ cup granulated sugar

½ cup dry white wine

2 Tbsp scented vinegar (pg. 32)

1 tsp sea salt

1 bay leaf

¼ tsp caraway seeds

2-inch long cinnamon stick

5 whole plum cloves

Dusting of white pepper

Procedure

Cut cabbage and apples into small chunks, mix in the lemon juice and set aside. Combine bacon and grape seed oil in saucepan and crisp the bacon over high heat. Add the minced garlic and lightly brown. Add the onions and lightly sweat them. Add the cabbage, apples and lemon juice and mix ingredients well. Add the sugar, wine, vinegar, salt, and all spices. Mix well and bring to a boil. Reduce heat, cover the saucepan and braise the cabbage. Stir occasionally so it doesn't burn. Gently braise it until cabbage leaves are tender, but not mushy! (Remove cinnamon stick, cloves, and bay leaf before serving if so desired.)

A WORD OF CAUTION: Do not overcook red cabbage. It will lose texture, flavor, and color.

High School

One of the hardest things in any kid's life is navigating the changes that come with high school. I had the pleasure of further complicating this time in my life with a fulltime job working in a high-stress environment, for my parents. My mom and dad were never sure about some of my friends, but recognizing that we lived in a remote location, and there were not a lot of other options, they resigned to the fact that my friends were my friends.

One of my best friends had a penchant for entertaining a crowd, making friends in any environment, and making people question his intellect and sanity. This is exactly the type of person my father was most concerned about me associating with.

On one particularly stressful evening at the restaurant, in the midst of the 7:30 dinner rush, and at a time when you could cut the tension (or a waiter) with a knife, Ken walked in. Dad muttered something not suitable for printing in a family cookbook, and cocked a suspicious glance. Ken, unfazed, walked in with his Mohawk haircut and said, "Yo! What's up Hermbud?!" My dad, for the first time in his life, was speechless (and I was scared ****less!).

Poached Apple Stars

YIELD: 4 servings

Ingredients

2 firm medium-size apples
½ cup fresh lemon juice
1 cup dry sparkling white wine

Procedure

Core apples. With a sharp, pointed paring knife, make 10 equal incisions to form a star-shaped pattern into the apple, being sure incisions go to the center of the apple. Carefully separate the pieces. You will get 2 stars per apple. Dip the stars meat-side down into the lemon juice to prevent discoloring. Place the stars in a poaching skillet and pour lemon juice and sparkling wine over them. Cover with a lid and gently poach the stars until they are soft to the touch, but still firm, about 8 minutes. Store them in the poaching liquid.

Adrieke and Chris, 1999

Entrées

The Fawn Brook Inn

Duck à L'Orange with Sauce Bigarade

YIELD: 4 servings

Ingredients

Very fine juliennes of fresh ginger
  (same amount as orange zest)

1 cup Grand Marnier liqueur, plus 2 oz

Zest of 1 large orange

4 duck breasts

¾ cup Sauce Bigarade (pg. 85)

4 square puff pastry shells (pg. 64)

Procedure

In a saucepan, combine the ginger and 1 cup Grand Marnier, and simmer until ginger is tender, about 5 minutes. Remove from heat and add the orange zest and the 2 oz Grand Marnier and marinate overnight.

Grill the duck breasts, fat side down, until the skin is crisp. Turn them over and grill them to medium rare. Slice each breast into thin medallions without cutting them all the way through—they need to stay in one solid piece. Drain the ginger and orange zest, reserving the liqueur. Heat the Sauce Bigarade in a skillet and add the breasts. Flambé with the reserved liqueur. Place duck breasts and sauce into warm crisp pastry shells and garnish with orange zest and ginger.

Sauce Bigarade for Duck à L'Orange

YIELD: ¾ cup, approximately 4 servings

Ingredients

8 oz Gewürztraminer wine

4 oz verjus (pg. 32)

1 oz balsamic vinegar

1 cup fresh orange juice

½ cup Grand Marnier liqueur

2 Tbsp fresh lime juice

1 Tbsp dark rum

3 oz fine granulated sugar

2 cups Demi-glace (pg. 21)

Procedure

In a saucepan combine the wine, verjus, vinegar, orange juice, Grand Marnier, lime juice, and rum and bring to a scalding point. Do not let it boil. In a medium-size saucepan add the sugar and carefully caramelize to a very light brown color. Carefully incorporate the hot liquid, one ladle at a time, to the sugar, adjusting the heat as necessary. Keep stirring until all of the caramelized sugar is completely dissolved.

Lower heat and reduce the mixture to half its volume. In a small saucepan bring Demi-glace to a boil, then combine it with the caramelized liquid and simmer gently until volume is reduced in half again.

Sam and Annette Siegel adopted the Groicher's into their family.

Veal Rouladen "Swiss Style"

YIELD: 4 servings

Ingredients

8 slices of veal loin, each weighing about 3 oz

3 Tbsp Italian parsley, chopped

2 Tbsp thyme leaves

1 Tbsp lemon grass, finely chopped

2 Tbsp chives, chopped

1 tsp salt

1 tsp pepper

1 Tbsp black truffle oil

8 slices of brie cheese

Dusting of white flour

½ cup garlic butter (pg. 30)

½ cup extra virgin olive oil

3 oz sweet Vermouth

2 cups ripe tomatoes, peeled, deseeded, and finely cubed

4 Tbsp fresh basil, chopped

2 Tbsp crème fraîche (pg. 25)

1½ cups Demi-glace (pg. 21)

Procedure

Flatten out the veal slices to ½-inch thickness. In a bowl combine the parsley, thyme, lemon grass, chives, salt, pepper, and the black truffle oil. Work mixture into a paste and season each veal slice with it. Place a slice of brie on each veal slice and roll it up tightly. Tuck in the ends and secure each roll with a toothpick. Pass each roll through the flour. In a skillet combine garlic butter and olive oil and bring it to a bubbling point. Brown each rouladen evenly on all sides. Carefully deglaze the pan with the Vermouth. Remove the meat from the skillet and keep warm in a warm oven. Add the tomatoes to the skillet and soften them in the hot oil. Add the basil, swirl in the crème fraîche and the Demi-glace, and bring it back to a bubbling point. Add the warm veal rolls. Cover the skillet with a lid and gently simmer the dish for about 8 minutes. When serving, remove the toothpicks from the rouladens. Serve with buttered noodles.

MSG

God did not invent it, nor do I use it. It is simply a slow-working poison.

Chicken Cordon Bleu

YIELD: 4 servings

Ingredients

4 8-oz boneless, skinless chicken breasts

4 oz ham, finely sliced

4 1-oz slices of Gouda or Swiss Emmenthal cheese

2 whole large eggs

2 egg yolks

Pinch of salt

½ cup all-purpose white flour

2 cups fine bread crumbs

8 oz (1 cup) melted butter, clarified (pg. 27)

½ cup grape seed oil

Procedure

Butterfly the breasts and carefully flatten them out to about ⅛-inch thick, keeping the breast in one piece. Evenly distribute the ham and the cheese to each breast and flap the breasts back together. In a bowl, whisk the eggs, egg yolks, and salt until well combined. Dredge each breast individually with flour, shaking off all excess, then dip them in the egg mixture. Be sure entire breast is coated well. Lastly, coat them with the breadcrumbs. Gently and carefully press in the breadcrumbs with the palm of your hand. The entire breast needs to be completely covered with the crumbs.

In two skillets large enough to hold 2 breasts each, evenly distribute the butter and oil and bring to a bubbling point over high heat. Carefully place the breasts into the skillets—butter will splatter and can cause burns on skin. Lightly brown them on one side. Turn them over, and repeat procedure twice. They need to be nicely browned on each side. Browning time is 5 to 8 minutes. Serve Cordon Bleus with lemon garnish, anchovy filets, and crème fraîche, if so desired.

Escalope de Veau "Viennoise"

YIELD: 4 servings

Ingredients

16 oz trimmed veal loin

3 whole eggs

5 egg yolks

1 tsp salt

½ tsp lemon pepper (pg. 13)

¾ cup all-purpose white flour

3 cups fine breadcrumbs

16 oz clarified butter (pg. 27)

8 oz grape seed oil

Lingonberries (see below)

Procedure

Slice veal into 2-ounce escalopes (strips). With a meat mallet, flatten them out to about ⅛-inch thick. In a bowl, combine the eggs and egg yolks, season with salt and pepper, and whisk until well combined. Generously dust each escalope on both sides with flour. Pass them through the egg wash, shaking off all excess liquid. Pass them through the breadcrumbs, gently pressing them into the escalopes and being sure both sides are well covered with crumbs.

In a large enough skillet to hold 2 escalopes, bring 4 ounces of the clarified butter and 2 ounces grape seed oil to a bubbling point. Carefully place escalopes into it and over high heat sauté both sides to golden brown. Remove from skillet and keep warm in a slow oven. Discard the butter/oil mixture. Add 4 more ounces of clarified butter and 2 ounces of grape seed oil and bring to a bubbling point. Repeat procedure for the rest of the escalopes. Serve the escalopes with lemon wedges and a bowl of lingonberries.

Lingonberries

YIELD: 1 cup

Ingredients

1 cup fresh or frozen lingonberries;
   if frozen be sure they are thawed and drained of all liquids

1 cup Apple Glace (pg. 29)

Combine berries and apple glace and refrigerate.

Black Forest Beef Rouladen

YIELD: 4 servings

Ingredients

3 oz smoked lean bacon, diced

3 oz shallots, minced

2 oz garlic (approximately 2 cloves), finely minced

4 cornichons (baby gherkins) approximately 1 oz, finely diced

6 plump juniper berries, crushed

¼ tsp whole caraway seeds

8 4-oz beef filets, butterflied

Dijon mustard

Dusting of freshly ground white pepper

½ cup olive oil

All-purpose white flour

2 oz Cabernet Sauvignon or Pinot Noir wine

Procedure

In a skillet, combine 1 Tbsp olive oil and bacon. Crisp the bacon over high heat. Reduce heat and add the shallots, garlic, and cornichons. Sauté just enough until shallots are al dente. Add the crushed juniper berries and caraway seeds. Combine well. Strain the mixture through a fine wire-mesh sieve. Reserve the oil and bacon drippings.

With a meat tenderizer, gently flatten the filets to about ⅛-inch thick, preventing any holes from forming in the meat. Very lightly coat each one with Dijon mustard, dust them with freshly ground white pepper, and distribute the drained bacon mixture on each filet. Carefully and tightly roll each one up, closing up ends so stuffing cannot fall out. Secure each one with a toothpick to prevent unrolling during cooking procedure.

In a large enough frying skillet, combine the reserved bacon and oil drippings with ½ cup olive oil and bring to a low boil. Reduce heat slightly to prevent splashing and burns. Dredge the rouladen through the white flour, shaking off excess flour. Place them into the hot oil and nicely brown them on all sides, about 12 to 15 minutes. Adjust heat according to need. Drain off all cooking oil (leave rouladen in pan). Reduce heat to very low, and while skillet is still hot, carefully but quickly deglaze the pan with the red wine. Use extreme caution if an open gas flame is the cooking media.

Rouladen Sauce

1 cup Demi-glace (pg. 21)

¼ cup crème fraîche (pg. 25)

1 tsp smooth Dijon mustard

Combine all 3 ingredients. Mix well and pour over the rouladen. Cover sauce pan with a lid and very gently simmer for about 15 minutes. Carefully remove toothpicks before serving.

Sweetbreads "Fawn Brook"

YIELD: 2 servings

Ingredients

14 oz sweetbreads

1 lemon

1 bay leaf

2 Tbsp black truffle oil

1 small shallot diced (about ¾ oz)

2 small cloves of garlic, finely chopped

½ cup Madeira Sauce (pg. 21)

1 tsp pink peppercorns

2 slivers of black truffle, coarsely chopped

2 sprigs Italian parsley, chopped

½ cup Demi-glace (pg. 21)

2 Tbsp crème fraîche (pg. 25)

Pinch of kosher salt, if needed

3 Tbsp olive oil

4 medium-sized shiitake mushrooms
(about 3 oz) 2 sliced, 2 whole

4 oz foie gras mousse

1 pinch lavender flowers

2 4-oz baked puff pastry shells (pg. 64)

Procedure

To poach the sweetbreads: Season water with a pinch of salt, a quarter of a lemon, and a bay leaf. Bring to a boil and plunge the raw sweetbreads into it. Reduce the heat and simmer them for 15 to 20 minutes. Check for doneness. They should be slightly pink inside, but not bloody. Immediately place them in iced water. Cool and peel them while still warm. Gently break them in pieces, removing all fat, tissues, and skin. Keep them under refrigeration until ready for use.

In a skillet, heat the truffle oil and lightly glaze the shallots and garlic. Add the Madeira and pink peppercorns. With gentle heat, reduce the liquid to about 2 tablespoons. Add the chopped truffles, parsley, and Demi-glace. Keep the sauce at simmering point for about 10 minutes. Add the crème fraîche and combine well. Taste the sauce for correct seasoning. Add a little salt if needed.

In a separate skillet, heat the olive oil. Add the mushrooms, sliced and whole, and lightly sauté. Remove the whole mushrooms for garnish. Add the foie gras mousse and mix well.

Add the sweetbreads and lavender flowers and mix well. Add the prepared sauce, cover the skillet with a lid, and simmer the dish just enough until the sweetbreads are heated through. *A word of caution:* Do not overcook the sweetbreads as they have a tendency to become rubbery, chewy, and quite tough. Preheat the pastry shells, then fill with the sweetbreads and garnish with mushroom caps.

Goulash

YIELD: 4 servings

Ingredients

20 oz lean beef, cubed

Dusting of white flour

Dusting of sweet paprika

½ tsp salt

Dusting of black pepper

¼ cup grape seed oil

5 oz bacon, chopped

1 oz garlic, minced

4 oz onions, diced

1 small red bell pepper,
de-seeded and chopped

1 medium ripe tomato, chopped

¼ tsp thyme leaves

2 bay leaves

2 Tbsp sweet paprika

1 cup Riesling wine

1 cup beef stock (pg. 20)

1 cup heavy cream

1 cup crème fraîche (pg. 25)

Roux if so desired (pg. 21)

Procedure

Dust cubed beef with flour, paprika, salt, and pepper. In a skillet combine grape seed oil with bacon and set over high heat. Crisp the bacon, add minced garlic and lightly brown. Add the onions and bell pepper and lightly sweat them. Add the beef cubes with the flour and paprika and brown the cubes on all sides. Add the tomatoes, thyme, bay leaves, and paprika and combine well. Add the wine and beef stock and combine well. Add the cream and crème fraîche and combine well. Bring it to a boil. Reduce the heat and simmer the stew until the meat is nice and tender. If using pot roast simmer for 2 to 3 hours. If using filet simmer for about 15 minutes. If so desired, lightly thicken it with roux.

Grandkids Cayden and Anneliese

Sauerbraten

YIELD: 4 servings

Ingredients

2 lb rib roast

1 oz garlic, diced fine

1 Tbsp brown sugar

1 Tbsp kosher salt

3 Tbsp olive oil

Marinade ingredients:

½ tsp black peppercorns

½ tsp juniper berries

½ tsp allspice

½ tsp cinnamon

2 oz carrot, coarsely chopped

2 oz celery, coarsely chopped

2 oz onion, coarsely chopped

2 oz turnip, coarsely chopped

Few sprigs parsley, coarsely chopped

Few sprigs lovage, coarsely chopped

1 tsp whole cloves

1 tsp yellow mustard seed

1 tsp caraway seed

Few bay leaves, crumbled

1 cup water

1 cup red wine

½ cup wine vinegar

2 Tbsp grape seed oil

Procedure

Work garlic, sugar, salt, and olive oil into a paste. Rub the paste onto the roast and set aside. Combine the peppercorns, juniper berries, allspice, and cinnamon and pound into a coarse consistency. Combine all the chopped vegetables, seasonings, wine, water, and vinegar into a saucepan. Bring to a boil and then reduce the heat and simmer for 20 minutes. Remove from heat and let it cool to lukewarm.

Pour marinade over the seasoned roast. Cover and refrigerate for 5 days, turning the roast over once a day. Once the roast has marinated for 5 days, remove and pat dry with paper towels. Do not discard marinade.

(continued)

Place 2 tablespoons grape seed oil in a skillet over high heat. When oil is bubbling, carefully add the roast and brown all sides. Drain the vegetables from the marinade and place them in a roasting pan with 1 cup of the marinade liquid. Place the meat on top of the vegetables and cover pan with foil. Place in a preheated oven at 450 degrees for 1 hour and 30 minutes. Remove the foil and crisp the outside of the roast for another 30 minutes. Remove roast from the pan and cover to keep warm. Discard vegetables. Drain the juices from the pan and degrease for making the Gingersnap Sauce (see below). There should be about 1½ cups.

Gingersnap Sauce
Ingredients

1 ½ cups pan juices

½ cup Demi-glace (pg. 21)

1 oz gingersnaps, crumbled

2 Tbsp crème fraîche (pg. 25)

Procedure

Place the pan juices over high heat and reduce to about 1 cup. Add the Demi-glace and mix well. Simmer for about 15 minutes. Add the crumbled gingersnaps and whisk until sauce has a smooth and silky texture. Whisk in the crème fraîche.

Garnish for the Sauerbraten:

Crisp Potato Pancakes (pg. 74)

Apple Stars filled with lingonberries or red currant jelly (pg. 82)

Red Cabbage (pg. 81)

Gingersnap Sauce (see above)

Assembly of Sauerbraten:

Slice the roast against the grain into thin slices. Place on a serving platter and lightly pour some Gingersnap Sauce over the slices. Arrange potato pancakes on one side and sprinkle lightly with fresh chopped parsley. Fill the center of apple stars with lingonberries or currant jelly and place around the roast. Serve with a side of red cabbage and the rest of the Gingersnap Sauce.

Roasted Turkey with Apricot-Chestnut Dressing

YIELD: 6–7 servings

Ingredients

1 turkey, approximately 12–14 lbs (about 1 lb per person)

1 medium leek

1 celery heart

1 large carrot

1 large onion

3 large ripe tomatoes

1 medium turnip

Few sprigs rosemary

3–4 bay leaves, crushed

8–10 whole cloves

Seasonings:

4 large cloves of garlic, finely chopped

1 Tbsp salt

1 tsp freshly ground pepper (preferably white pepper)

1 oz fresh sage, finely chopped

6 juniper berries, crushed

Apricot-Chestnut Stuffing (see next page)

1 cup Madeira wine or cream sherry

Procedure

Rinse leek, celery, carrot, onion, tomatoes, and turnip in cold water and coarsely chop. Place into a deep roasting pan. Season the vegetables with rosemary, bay leaves, and cloves. In a bowl combine seasonings and mix well. Clean the bird and rub the seasonings on both the inside and outside. Stuff the bird tightly with the Apricot Chestnut stuffing and place it on top of the vegetables. Lightly prick the skin on the breast numerous time with a skewer, then pour 1 cup of Madeira or cream sherry over it.

Cover the roasting pan with aluminum foil and roast in a preheated oven at 450 degrees for 3 hours. Uncover the bird and bake at 400 degrees for another 30 to 40 minutes to brown the skin. Brush the skin frequently with a mixture of melted butter mixed with Madeira. To check for doneness of the bird, insert a skewer into the breast and if the juices coming out are a pinkish white color, the bird is done. DO NOT overroast it. The meat will become quite dry and tasteless. Remove the bird from the roasting pan and keep it warm in a warm oven. Discard vegetables. Strain all the roasting juices through a fine wire-mesh sieve. Use the juices to make the sauce below.

Turkey Sauce
Ingredients

2 cups roasting juices, fat removed

1 cup chicken stock (pg. 20)

1 cup tomato juice

1 cup sour cream

8–10 gingersnaps

Procedure

In a saucepan, combine the roasting juices, chicken broth, and tomato juice and bring to a low boil. Whisk in the sour cream. Crumble the ginger-snaps to lightly thicken the sauce. Whisk until sauce has a smooth and silky texture.

Apricot-Chestnut Stuffing
Ingredients

8 oz dried apricots, julienned

1 lb chestnuts, peeled and precooked

¼ cup apricot liqueur

½ cup pure maple syrup

½ cup heavy cream

½ cup chicken stock (pg. 20)

2 large whole eggs

3 large egg yolks

8 oz crusty white bread, cubed

½ cup olive oil

½ cup chives, chopped

½ cup fresh sage, coarsely chopped

Pinch of salt

Freshly ground white pepper

Procedure

In a skillet combine the apricots, chestnuts, liqueur, and syrup. Bring to a boil, then turn off heat. Let the apricots and chestnuts soak in the hot liquid. In a mixing bowl combine the cream, chicken stock, eggs, and egg yolks and whip until frothy. Pour over the cubed bread and mix well. In a small skillet lightly sauté the chives and sage in olive oil. Mix into bread mixture. Add the cooled apricot-chestnut mixture to the bread and mix well. Season with salt and pepper to taste. Stuffing is now ready for the bird.

Truite au Bleu (Blaue Forelle)

YIELD: 2 servings

Ingredients

2 fresh trout, about 10 oz each   hot melted butter

court bouillon (see below)   cold dill sauce (pg. 26)

parsley

Court Bouillon:

Do not use an aluminum cooking pot!

4 cups cold water   ½ medium lemon

2 whole bay leaves   1 cup dry white wine

1 Tbsp salt

Procedure

IT IS ESSENTIAL TO USE LIVE TROUT IN THIS RECIPE!

Kill the trout at the last minute before cooking. They must be cleaned quickly without handling them too much. It is the film of slime that covers the fish that will give them the blue color.

Plunge them into the boiling court bouillon at once, being sure they are completely submerged, and lightly poach them for about 10 minutes. They will curl up and take on a light blue hue. Blue trout need to be served immediately as they quickly turn black by being exposed to air.

Serve them with new potatoes sprinkled with parsley, hot melted butter, and cold dill sauce.

Pan-fried Trout "Almondine"

YIELD: One 10 oz trout per serving

Ingredients

10 oz almond butter (pg. 30)   Parsley

1 Tbsp blanched, sliced almonds   Chives

Lemon wedges

Procedure

In a skillet pan-fry the cleaned fresh trout in almond butter (or olive oil) on both sides until done. Add sliced almonds and season with lemon wedges, freshly chopped parsley and chives. Serve the trout with the lightly burned butter.

Vegetarian Strudel

YIELD: 4 servings

Ingredients

1½ oz shallots, diced

½ oz garlic, minced

½ oz fresh ginger, peeled and minced

½ cup grape seed oil

1 large Portobello mushroom
(approximately 4 oz), sliced

4 oz roasted pimientos, julienned

1 cup sundried tomatoes purchased in oil

4 oz fresh asparagus tips,
approximately 5 inches long

4 oz baby artichokes, quartered

1 cup pitted black olives

¼ cup pine nuts, lightly roasted

¼ cup sundried blueberries

Salt and pepper to taste

6 oz puff pastry (pg. 64)

Egg wash (pg. 3)

Cream of Mascarpone (see below)

Procedure

In a skillet, lightly sauté shallots, garlic, and ginger in the grape seed oil. Add sliced Portobello mushroom and lightly sauté. Add the julienned pimientos, sundried tomatoes, asparagus tips, quartered artichokes, olives, pine nuts, and sundried blueberries. Season with salt and pepper. Combine all ingredients well and warm entire mixture. Do not cook it or boil it. Place contents into a strainer and drain off all the liquid.

Place puff pastry on a double-folded piece of parchment paper and dust lightly with flour. Roll it out to a 9 x 8-inch rectangle and evenly distribute the mixture, leaving approximately a ½-inch border of puff pastry free on the farthest end away from you. Carefully roll up the strudel, being sure the seam is on the bottom. Tuck in all the contents and seal off the ends. Transfer the strudel with the parchment paper underneath onto a metal sheet pan. Brush with the egg wash and poke a few holes into the top of the strudel with a fork, allowing steam to escape. Bake in a preheated oven at 450 degrees for approximately 20 minutes, then rotate the pan and bake for an additional 15 minutes, or until the strudel is a nicely golden brown.

Cream of Mascarpone for Vegetarian Strudel

YIELD: 1+ cup

Ingredients

¾ cup mascarpone, at room temperature

¼ cup crème fraîche (pg. 25)

2 oz goat cheese, at room temperature

¼ tsp Maharajah curry powder

¼ tsp chives, chopped

Pinch of dill

¼ tsp fresh lime juice

Salt and pepper to taste

Pinch of saffron

Procedure

Combine mascarpone, crème fraîche, and goat cheese. Mix it well until no lumps remain in the sauce. Whisk in all ingredients, except saffron. With a spatula, fold in the saffron. Let the sauce stand for approximately 30 minutes. Place sauce into a pastry bag fitted with a small star tip. Pipe out small rosettes, each weighing approximately ½ ounce, or about the size of a quarter. Refrigerate and serve with hot strudel.

Rack of Lamb

YIELD: 4 servings

Ingredients

4 14-oz loin racks of lamb

Seasonings:

2 Tbsp garlic, minced	1 Tbsp kosher salt
2 Tbsp chives, chopped	Dusting of white pepper
2 Tbsp parsley, chopped	4 Tbsp olive oil
1 tsp rosemary leaves	Rack of Lamb Sauce (see below)
2 Tbsp smooth Dijon mustard	

Procedure

Have your butcher french and trim the lamb for you. Loosen the meat from the ribcage, leaving just enough meat on the bone to hold the loin in place. Mix the seasonings and rub on the inside of the loin and replace the meat. Add the salt and pepper to the mixture and rub the rest on the outside of the rack. Place the racks in a deep roasting pan so that they are not touching. Coat each rack with a tablespoon of olive oil. Roast them in high heat of 485 degrees to medium rare, about 25 minutes.

Rack of Lamb Sauce
Ingredients

1 Tbsp garlic, finely minced	1 tsp fresh thyme leaves
1 Tbsp shallots, finely minced	¼ cup pinot noir wine
½ tsp cracked green peppercorns	½ cup Demi-glace (pg. 21)
½ tsp cracked pink peppercorns	1 tsp crème fraîche (pg. 25)
2 Tbsp black truffle oil	1½ oz Armagnac brandy

Procedure

In a skillet large enough to hold the 4 racks, combine garlic, shallots, peppercorns, and the truffle oil. Over high heat, glaze garlic and shallots to transparent stage. Add the thyme leaves and the wine and reduce to half its volume until a somewhat syrup stage is achieved. Add the Demi-glace and crème fraîche. Swirl it and bring it to boiling point. Add the roasted loin racks to it and quickly flambé with the Armagnac. Serve the racks with a dash of sauce and minted raspberry jelly.

Steak au Poivre

YIELDS: 4 servings

Ingredients

4 8-oz filets

1½ oz elephant garlic,
   shaved to a fine consistency

Dusting of sea salt

Few drops of black truffle oil

1 Tbsp garlic butter (pg. 30)

1 Tbsp extra virgin olive oil

3 Tbsp shallots, finely minced

1½ tsp each green, pink, and
   szechuan peppercorns, slightly mashed

1 cup Madeira Sauce (pg. 21)

1 Tbsp crème fraîche (pg. 25)

1½ oz Armagnac brandy

Procedure

Butterfly the filets; gently rub the shaved garlic onto the inside of filets. Dust with salt and sprinkle black truffle oil. Fold steaks back together and grill to less than desired doneness. Do not cook all the way as they will be finished off in the skillet.

In a skillet large enough to hold the four steaks, heat the garlic butter and olive oil. Add the shallots and sauté until lightly toasted. Add the peppercorns, Madeira sauce, and crème fraîche. Bring to a boil and swirl the sauce to combine well. Place the filets into the sauce and finish cooking to desired temperature. Carefully flambé the steaks with the Armagnac. Serve filets lightly topped with the sauce. Serve the rest of the sauce on the side.

Tournedos Rossini

YIELD: 4 servings

Ingredients

4 8-oz beef filets

Sprinkle of black truffle oil
   for each steak, plus 1 Tbsp

Dusting of salt and pepper

2 oz sliced foie gras per steak (pg. 102)

1½ cups Demi-glace (pg. 21)

¼ cup Madeira wine

4 thin slices of black truffle

Procedure

Butterfly each filet, lightly brush them with black truffle oil, and dust with salt and pepper. Place on a hot grill and lightly grill them to almost medium rare or almost desired doneness. Remove from grill and place a slice of foie gras on each steak. Finish them in a hot 450-degree oven for just a few minutes. In a saucepan whisk the Madeira and 1 tablespoon black truffle oil into the Demi-glace and bring to a boil. Lightly simmer it down to about 1½ cups. Place a slice of black truffle on each steak, pour the finished sauce around the steaks, and serve remaining sauce separately.

Medallions of Veal "Normandy"

YIELD: 4 servings

Ingredients

3 oz garlic butter (pg. 30)

2 Tbsp extra virgin olive oil

8 large shiitake mushrooms, stems removed

16 oz veal tenderloin

4 tsp black truffle oil

Dusting of coarse kosher salt

4 Tbsp chives, finely chopped

1 tsp lemon grass, finely chopped

½ tsp lavender flowers

2 Tbsp sundried blueberries, firmly packed

1 tsp each of green, pink, and szechuan peppercorns

2 cups of Demi-glace with a few drops of black truffle oil (pg. 21)

2 Tbsp crème fraîche (pg. 25)

1 oz calvados and 1 tsp 151 rum, combined

Procedure

One day ahead, combine garlic butter and olive oil in skillet. Bring to bubbling point and lightly sauté mushrooms. Place mushroom cups and oil in a container and refrigerate overnight.

Trim the tenderloin of all fat and silver skin. Butterfly into 8 equal medallions. Brush veal medallions with black truffle oil and dust with salt. On a hot grill, brown them on both sides to medium rare or desired doneness. Place oil and garlic butter from mushroom cups into a skillet and bring to bubbling point. Add the chives, lemon grass, and lavender flowers and lightly sweat. Add the blueberries and the peppercorns. Add the Demi-glace and crème fraîche and combine the sauce well. Simmer it for a few minutes, stirring it so the oil and sauce are well combined. Gently heat the mushroom cups in a separate skillet. Add the veal medallions to the sauce in the skillet and bring to a boil. Carefully ignite the dish with the calvados-rum mixture. Add the mushroom cups to the dish and serve while hot.

Grandsons Alex and Nicholas

Chateau Briand

YIELDS: 2 servings

Ingredients

1 tsp extra virgin olive oil
1 Tbsp shallots, minced
1 tsp garlic, minced
1 tsp green and pink pepper corns,
   lightly smashed
½ cup Demi-glace (pg. 21)
1 oz red wine

16 oz center-cut beef filet
Dash of freshly ground
   white pepper and kosher salt
1 tsp black truffle oil
½ oz cognac
½ cup Sauce Béarnaise (pg. 27)

Procedure

In a skillet, heat olive oil, add shallots and garlic and lightly sauté. Add the smashed peppercorns, Demi-glace, and red wine and slightly reduce. Rub the filet with pepper, salt, and truffle oil. Grill meat on all sides to desired doneness. Place meat into the simmering sauce and carefully flambé with the cognac. Slice meat into four equal portions and serve with warm Sauce Béarnaise.

Shrimp Provencale

YIELD: 4 servings

Ingredients

1½ cups garlic butter (pg. 30)
12 jumbo Tiger shrimp
Freshly squeezed lemon juice
1 cup extra virgin olive oil
2 Tbsp shallots, minced

1 cup fresh ripe tomatoes, diced
4 large shiitake mushrooms,
   stems removed
1 Tbsp fresh parsley, chopped
Dash of lavender flowers

Procedure

Butterfly and devein the shrimp. The shells should be left intact on the shrimp, as they will keep the shrimp juicy and succulent during cooking procedure. In a large skillet melt the garlic butter and add the shrimp standing up with the flesh side down. Cover skillet with a lid and sauté over moderate-high heat for a few minutes. Check for doneness—shrimp should have a very light pale hue and the shells should turn to a very light pink color. *Do NOT overcook them.* Sprinkle a few drops of lemon juice over them and add lavender flowers. In a separate skillet bring the olive oil to a bubbling point and add the minced shallots. Sauté al dente. Add the diced tomatoes and mushroom cups. Sauté the mushrooms to a soft stage. Sprinkle the parsley over them, then arrange shrimp on serving plates. Garnish with the mushroom cups and ladle the tomatoes over them. Serve with hot butter on the side.

Beef Wellington

YIELDS: 2 servings

Ingredients

16 oz center-cut beef filet

Dash of freshly ground white pepper and kosher salt

1 tsp black truffle oil

5 oz puff pastry (pg. 64)

4 oz foie gras mousse (see below)

Egg wash (pg. 3)

4 oz of Demi-glace with a few drops of black truffle oil (pg. 21)

Procedure

Lightly rub the filet with salt, pepper, and black truffle oil. Grill the meat on all sides to almost the desired doneness, but preferably rare. Do not overcook as the meat will cook some more in the oven. Cut out three small leaf designs from the edge of the puff pastry and set aside. Place the foie gras mousse in the center of the pastry and place the filet on top. Carefully wrap the pastry around it. Place the wrapped filet in a well-greased baking dish with the seams down. Brush with egg wash, decorate with the cutout leaves, and place in a preheated oven at 485 degrees for about 18 minutes or until the pastry is golden brown. Slice the Wellington into 4 equal portions and serve it with hot black truffle oil-infused Demi-glace on the side.

Foie Gras (Goose Liver)

YIELD: approximately 14–16 oz

Ingredients

14–16 oz goose liver (use only grade A or B)

3 cups dry white wine

1 tsp salt

In a mortar, crack:

4 cloves

¼ tsp black peppercorns

3 allspice berries

Procedure

In a saucepan add salt and spices to wine and bring to a boil; reduce heat. Immerse the liver into the liquid and very gently poach the liver to *medium rare.* Turn the liver once during poaching time. *Do NOT boil the liver at any time,* it could disintegrate or fall apart. Place a wire rack on a sheet pan and gently place poached liver on it to cool. Save all fat and juice extract while liver is cooling.

(continued)

Mousse de Fois Gras

YIELD: approximately 2½ cups

Ingredients

Fat and juices extracted from the cooling liver (previous page)

2 Tbsp black truffle oil

½ oz garlic, finely minced

3 oz shiitake mushroom cups, sliced

Dusting of fresh thyme leaves

¼ tsp salt

¼ tsp fresh ground black pepper

Cooled poached goose liver

1 Tbsp truffle peelings

½ cup port

Procedure

In a skillet bring the truffle oil and extracted liver fat to a bubbling point. Add the minced garlic and lightly brown. Add the mushrooms, sauté them, and season with the thyme, salt, and pepper. Cube the poached liver and save all the drippings that escape while doing the chopping. Combine the liver with its drippings, and the mushrooms with all the juices and oils. Add the truffle peelings and the port. Mix well and place all of it into a food processor. Puree it to a fine, smooth consistency. Immediately refrigerate for future use. If properly packed, the mousse can also be frozen up to six months. Mousse may also be obtained in specialty food stores.

Marinated Jumbo Sea Scallops

YIELD: 4 Servings

Ingredients

32 oz of scallops (4 jumbo sea scallops
    per person, approx 8 oz each)

1 tsp kosher salt

¼ cup fresh squeezed lime juice

1 cup dry sparkling wine

Procedure

Place scallops in a glass or stainless steel container. Sprinkle with salt, add the lime juice and the sparkling wine, being sure the scallops are completely submerged in the liquid. Add more sparkling wine if needed. Cover airtight and refrigerate 48 hours before use. Scallops will keep safely for up to 2 weeks under proper refrigeration.

As the scallops are marinating, they are also cooking at the same time and may be eaten as is, with a delicate cold curry sauce (page 25) or Sauce Remoulade (page 25), or as sushi to your liking. As a word of caution, when cooking them, just slightly warm them in hot butter with your preference of seasoning and oil. Please keep in mind, if overcooked they will turn to rubber.

Lobster Thermidor
YIELD: 4 servings

Ingredients

4 4-oz cold-water rock lobster tails

Boiling, lightly salted lemon water

8 oz baby langoustines (prawns)

1 oz butter

2 Tbsp shallots, finely minced

1 tsp lemon grass, finely chopped

¼ cup dry white wine

2 tsp smooth Dijon mustard

A dash of salt

A dash of cayenne pepper

1 tsp chervil, chopped

1½ cup Thermidor Sauce (pg. 23)

3 oz grated gruyere cheese

Lemon slices for garnish

Black olives for garnish

Procedure

Carefully remove the meat from the lobster tails; if possible keep the shells intact. Remove the intestines from the tail meat, poach the tail meat and the shells in boiling salted lemon water, just long enough for the tail meat to turn transparent white in the center. Immediately cool them off in iced water. Reserve the shells; slice the tail meat into 3 or 4 medallions.

Combine the medallions and baby langoustines and set aside. In a saucepan, melt the butter and lightly brown the shallots and lemon grass, carefully add the white wine and under gentle simmering, reduce it to one-third its volume. Add the mustard, salt, cayenne pepper, and chervil, reduce it just a tad more, then add the lobster medallions and baby langoustines. Mix in the Thermidor Sauce and just lightly heat it through. Fill the tails with the langoustines, place the lobster medallions in a nice decorative fashion on top, and finish it off with the sauce. Sprinkle lightly with the grated gruyere cheese. Brown it au gratin in a hot oven. Garnish with thinly sliced lemon quarters and thinly sliced black olive disks.

NOTE: if baby langoustines are not available, baby cocktail shrimp or cleaned fat-free crawfish tails can be substituted.

Seafood en "Brochette"

YIELD: 4 servings

Ingredients

1 lemon

8 shrimp (8 to 10 shrimp per lb)

4 4-oz cold-water lobster tails

8 jumbo marinated sea scallops (pg. 103)

8 oz cooked crawfish tails, cleaned

4 medium-size artichoke bottoms

1 cup hot lemon butter (pg. 30)

4 lemon wedges for garnish

1 recipe Sauce Hollandaise (pg. 27)

Procedure

Have two pots of salted water with lemon wedges ready. Lobster and shrimp have two very distinctive and different flavors; we do not want to mix them up. Also lobster tails take more time to poach. *A word of caution:* Seafood, if overcooked, can get quite tough and chewy. Not really pleasant to a gourmand's taste buds.

Clean, devein, and butterfly the shrimp and poach them just a few minutes until they take on a light white hue. Cool them off right away in iced water.

Carefully remove lobster tails from shell and poach in the boiling salted lemon water, again just a few minutes. The lobster meat should be transparent white in the center. Again cool them off immediately in iced water.

Assembly of Seafood en Brochette:
Place 1 shrimp on skewer followed by a scallop, place lobster tail in center followed by a scallop and finish off with the shrimp. Fill the artichoke bottom with the crawfish tail and place in the center of dinner plate. Place the skewered meat next to it and heat in a 450 degree preheated oven for about 8 minutes. Serve with individual servings of ¼ cup hot lemon butter, ¼ lemon wedge, and warm Sauce Hollandaise.

Alternative:
Lightly brush the brochette with grape seed oil and lightly toast it on a hot charcoal grill.

Again, a word of caution: Sauce Hollandaise, if exposed to a high heat source, will separate very quickly, so heat the sauce on low heat.

Kajetan and wife Kara

This is one of my favorite Fawn Brook memories, and one my wife would just as soon forget. Kara and I made many trips to Allenspark in the year before we married. On one of these occasions Kara decided to stay at the inn while I made a run into town with my Mom. Kara wanted to spend some time with my dad prepping for the evening dinner rush, and I was sure that I could count on dad to show her the finer points of running a restaurant.

Still, not wanting to be left out, I decided to add my own advice. I was on my way out the door and noticed that my dad had Kara separating eggs for making Hollandaise Sauce. Kara seemed a bit unsure of herself, even though she was doing exactly what was needed. Kara was about to ask what to do next with the eggs, and had I not gotten involved, she would have simply beat the eggs.

I explained to Kara that high-altitude cooking presents some challenges, and that making Hollandaise Sauce was one of those challenges. The eggs, I explained, could not be vigorously beaten, and a softer touch was needed. I told Kara that she should just gently break the yolks between her fingers, and gently mix the eggs together in the same manner. I had almost made it out the door when my dad came over, and softly inquired as to "what the hell" Kara was doing.

Filet of Pork "Calvados"

YIELD: 4 servings

Ingredients

2 pork tenderloins, each weighing about 1 lb

Zest of 1 lemon

1 tsp kosher salt

½ tsp fresh thyme leaves

A dusting of ground white pepper

6 oz chèvre cheese

1 medium-sized tart apple, cored, peeled, and sliced

A good sprinkle of black truffle oil and grape seed oil

½ cup Madeira wine

1½ cups Apple-Raspberry-Pepper Glace (pg. 29)

1½ oz calvados brandy

Procedure

Remove the silver skin from the tenderloins and split them length-wise in half, being sure tenderloin stays in one piece. Carefully pound them out to about ¼-inch thick. Season the meat with the lemon zest, salt, thyme leaves, and pepper. With a hot wet metal spatula spread out the chèvre cheese evenly, leaving ¼-inch free on the edges of the meat. Place the apples down the center and lightly roll the tenderloins up. Secure the seams with metal skewers.

Generously rub the tenderloins with the black truffle and grape seed oil. In a large hot skillet, nicely brown the meat on all sides. Place them into a roasting pan, add the Madeira wine and finish them in a preheated oven at 425 degrees for 15 to 20 minutes for medium doneness.

In a large skillet, heat the apple-raspberry-pepper glace, add half the calvados to it and just lightly reduce the sauce. Remove the tenderloins from the pan, remove the skewers, and cut each one diagonally into 4 equal pieces. Place them back into the reducing glace and flambé them with the rest of the calvados.

Red Snapper Filet "Maison"

YIELD: 4 servings

Ingredients

4 8-oz filets

4 Tbsp olive oil, plus more as needed

A dash of salt

A dusting of white pepper

A few drops of lemon juice for each filet

6 oz baby langoustines or lobster medallions

4 Tbsp chives, chopped

2 Tbsp parsley, chopped

Zest of 1 lemon

2 oz candied ginger, sliced

4 double-twisted lemon slices for garnish

1 cup of Roasted Pimiento–Ginger Sauce (pg. 26)

Procedure

Brush each filet with 1 Tbsp olive oil; lightly dust with salt and pepper. In a hot skillet sear each filet on both sides, adding more oil as needed. Reduce the heat and slowly finish the filets until they become "flakey"—do not overcook them. Sprinkle a few drops of lemon juice on each filet.

In a separate skillet, combine the baby langoustines with the chives, parsley, and lemon zest. Add a little olive oil (1 Tbsp) and just lightly heat the mixture through. Place equal amount on each filet. Add the ginger and finish the filets off in a hot oven (450 degrees) for just a few minutes. Garnish with lemon twist. Serve the pimiento sauce cold, on the side.

Cheese Fondue

YIELD: 4 servings

Ingredients

2 French baguettes, about 8 oz each, cut into bite-size pieces
For the Fondue:

8 oz Emmental cheese

8 oz Gruyère cheese

1 medium clove of garlic

2 cups dry white wine

2 tsp ground arrowroot

½ cup Kirschwasser brandy

Dusting of nutmeg

Dusting of white pepper

Procedure

Grate both cheeses. Shave the garlic and generously rub the inside of the fondue pot with it. Add the white wine and bring to a simmering point. Do not boil the wine. Slowly add the cheeses, continuously stirring with a wooden spoon. Bring it to a low bubbling point. Add arrowroot with the Kirschwasser and stir it into the bubbling fondue, incorporating well. Season the fondue with the nutmeg and pepper. Serve immediately. Keep it lightly bubbling during eating time. The crust forming at the bottom of the pot can be lightly loosened and passed around for extra eating pleasure. Serve the fondue with a shot of Kirschwasser, dry white wine, or hot tea. Roesti (pg. 109) and an assortment of fresh fruits, such as sliced tart apples, pears, melon slices, and green grapes, will complement any fondue evening.

Roesti—Roasted Potatoes

YIELD: 4 servings

Ingredients

24 oz potatoes, preferably Yukon gold

8 oz butter

6 oz white onions, finely sliced

2 Tbsp minced garlic, loosely packed

2 Tbsp parsley, chopped

Salt and pepper to taste

Procedure

Peel and shred potatoes. Plunge them right away into cold water to prevent discoloring. Drain potatoes and squeeze out all moisture. Place them between paper towels and dry them off. In a large enough skillet bring butter to bubbling point and lightly glaze the onions and garlic. Add the potatoes and nicely brown them on one side. Add the parsley and flip the potatoes over and brown the other side to a light crisp. Season with salt and pepper to taste. Slide them off to a warm serving dish and serve immediately with the fondue on the previous page.

Lobster Curry

YIELD: 4 servings

Ingredients

  2 oz sweet butter or extra virgin olive oil
  3 Tbsp shallots, diced
  1½ oz dry white wine
  1½ cup Saffron-Curry Sauce (pg. 24)
  1 Tbsp Crème Fraiche (pg. 25)
  1 Tbsp Maharahah curry powder
  2 Tbsp golden raisins
    8 oz cooked lobster medallions
    8 oz cooked lobster claw meat
    2 Tbsp crystalized ginger, chopped
  Coconut flakes
  1 cup Fruit Chutney (pg. 48)

Procedure

In a skillet bring butter or olive oil to a bubbling point, quickly add the diced shallots and just lightly brown them. Carefully deglaze with the white wine, and let mixture lightly boil for a few seconds. Add the curry sauce and crème fraiche, reduce the heat and just gently simmer the sauce. Incorporate the curry powder and the raisins, mix well, and add the lobster medallions and claw meat. Coat well with the sauce, being sure the meat chunks are hot all the way through, but do not boil. Gently add the ginger. Place in serving vessel, dust with coconut flakes, and serve immediately with fruit chutney on the side.

Curry of Jumbo Scallops

YIELD: 4 servings

Procedure

Use the same procedure as for Lobster Curry above, substituting 16 oz jumbo scallops instead of lobster. Great care must be taken to not overcook the fine texture of the scallops. Just a few degrees of too much heat will make them quite tough, chewy, and tasteless.

Seafood Crepes

YIELD: 4 servings

Ingredients

2 oz sweet butter or extra virgin olive oil

2 Tbsp chives, minced

1 Tbsp lemon grass, finely chopped

1 Tbsp parsley, minced

1½ cups Thermidor Sauce (pg. 23)

2 Tbsp Crème Fraiche (pg. 25)

1 Tbsp smooth Dijon mustard

4 oz cooked lobster medallions

4 oz cooked king crab meat

4 oz cooked baby shrimp

4 oz marinated sea scallops (pg. 103)

8 French crepes (pg. 66)

3 oz Gruyère cheese, grated

Procedure

In a skillet bring butter or oil to a bubbling point and lightly sweat the chives, lemon grass, and parsley. Add half of the Thermidor sauce, the crème fraiche, and mustard, and combine well. Add the lobster, crab meat, shrimp, and scallops, and heat it all through. Do not boil. Fill the crepes with the meats, roll them up and place back into the skillet. Pour the remaining Thermidor sauce over the crepes, sprinkle with Gruyère cheese, and finish off in a hot oven for about 5–7 minutes, or until the cheese is nicely melted.

Go Little Book, and wish to all,
Flowers in the garden, meat in the hall.
A bit of wine, a spice of wit,
A cabin and the trees enclosing it.
A living brook amongst flowers galore,
And beautiful people passing through this door.

Granddaughter Anneliese.

*Grandsons Alex, Cayden,
and Nicholas.*

Kajetan and family, Christmas 2007.

Complete Gourmet Dinners

Starting with an aperitif, appetizer, soup, salad, main entrée, wine selection, dessert, coffee, and after dinner drinks

The Fawn Brook Inn

**FAWN BROOK
FAMILY MEMORIES**

Lobster Racing

Every New Year, my dad would give my brother and I each a lobster. He would get huge boxes full of live lobster to prepare for the guests of the evening. To my brother and I, they were another "food" adventure we could take advantage of. We would go into the walk-in cooler, despite strict warning from our dad, and see which of our lobsters could make it across the cooler floor first. If that didn't do the trick, we would ever so carefully take off the rubber bands holding their claws and play cat-and-mouse with each other. We would both come out of the cooler with "self-inflicted" wounds from our lobster warriors.

DINNER ONE

CRABMEAT-LOBSTER CAKE WITH SAUCE BEURRE BLANC

APPETIZER: Country Game Pâté (pg. 40)
with Sauce Cumberland (pg. 22)
Sandeman Fino Sherry 1983

SOUP: Chicken Consommé (pg. 50)
with Spinach-Cheese Gnocchis (pg. 67)
Igler Pinot Blanc

SALAD: Garden-fresh Salad with Avocado, Melon,
and Balsamic Vinaigrette Dressing (pg. 33)
Crusty Italian bread and butter

ENTRÉE: Crabmeat and Lobster Cakes with
Sauce Beurre Blanc served with
Bamboo Rice with Crystallized Ginger (pg. 80),
Steamed Broccoli and Almond Butter (pg. 30)
Pio-Cesare Barolo 1998

DESSERT: Crème Brûlée (pg. 171)
Coffee and *Cognac*

Crabmeat and Lobster Cakes

YIELD: 4 servings, eight 4-oz cakes

Ingredients

8 oz King Crab meat

8 oz lobster meat

8 oz crayfish meat

Dusting of salt and ground white pepper

1 Tbsp fresh lime juice

⅓ cup celery hearts, chopped, loosely packed

⅓ cup leeks, pale inside leaves only, chopped

⅓ cup red sweet pepper, chopped

2 Tbsp parsley, chopped

¼ tsp thyme leaves

¼ tsp mace

Dusting of cayenne

2 large eggs, well beaten

3 Tbsp mayonnaise (pg. 25)

1 Tbsp Dijon mustard

1 cup fine breadcrumbs

½ cup grape seed oil

Sauce Beurre Blanc (pg. 24)

Procedure

In a bowl, combine all meats, and dust with salt and pepper. Add the lime juice, cover, and marinate in the refrigerator for about 4 hours. Drain off all liquids and mix in celery, leeks, red peppers, parsley, and thyme leaves. Add the mace and cayenne. Stir in the beaten eggs, mayonnaise, mustard, and breadcrumbs. Cover with a towel and let it rest for 30 minutes. Form eight 4-oz cakes. In a skillet heat the grape seed oil on high and carefully brown the cakes on both sides to a nice golden hue, 3 to 5 minutes. Serve with heated Sauce Beurre Blanc.

DINNER TWO

ROASTED RACK OF VEAL WITH DIJON MUSTARD SAUCE

APPETIZER: Coconut Shrimp with Coconut Curry Sauce
Champagne Cocktail

SOUP: Hot Cream of Potato-Leek Soup (pg. 55)

SALAD: Salad with Champagne-Mimosa Dressing
Butter Croissants (pg. 141) with Olive Oil

ENTRÉE: Roasted Rack of Veal with Dijon Mustard Sauce,
Potato Pancakes (pg. 74)
and Juliennes of Roasted Red Peppers (pg. 71)
St Emilion Chateau Soutard 1999

DESSERT: Swiss Meringue with Raspberry Chocolate Ice
Coffee and *Cockburn Port, Vintage 1986*

Champagne Cocktail
YIELD: 1 cocktail

Ingredients

1 white sugar cube

Few drops of Angostura Bitter

1 Tbsp cognac

3 oz champagne

Lemon rind twist

½ orange slice

Procedure

Place sugar cube in a champagne flute. Add the bitter and cognac. With a small spoon, smash the sugar. Fill the flute with champagne, twist lemon rind into it and garnish with an orange slice.

Cheers!

Shrimp Appetizer
YIELD: 4 servings

Ingredients

8 large shrimp, peeled, deveined, and butterflied

1 cup dry white wine

1 Tbsp coconut milk

Coconut Curry Sauce (see below)

Dash of black caviar as garnish

4 Lemon slices

Dusting of freshly grated coconut

Procedure

Very lightly poach the shrimp in the wine and coconut milk. Marinate in liquid overnight. Place a dollop of Coconut Curry Sauce in a plate and place 2 shrimp at the edge of the sauce. Add a dash of black caviar on the sauce and garnish with a twisted lemon slice and freshly grated coconut.

Coconut Curry Sauce
YIELD: 4 servings

Ingredients

½ cup mayonnaise (pg. 25)

¼ cup crème fraîche (pg. 25)

1 Tbsp coconut milk

½ tsp ginger, finely minced

Few threads of saffron

½ tsp curry powder

Few drops lime juice

Dash of salt

Grated coconut flakes

Procedure

Mix all ingredients except coconut flakes until well incorporated. Season with salt to taste, and sprinkle coconut flakes over the sauce.

Salad with Champagne-Mimosa Dressing

YIELD: 4 servings, about ¾ cup

Ingredients

¼ cup Fruit-scented Vinegar (pg. 32)

½ cup extra virgin olive oil

1 Tbsp rose petal syrup (pg. 29)

1 Tbsp orange zest

1 hard boiled egg,
  finely chopped

Procedure

Whisk together vinegar, oil, syrup, and zest. Salt and pepper to taste. Arrange green salad leaves with various garnishes, drizzle dressing onto it, and finish with the chopped egg.

Rack of Veal

YIELD: 4 servings

Ingredients

4 lb veal rib rack with 4 rib bones

1 Tbsp garlic, finely minced

1 Tbsp chives, finely minced

1 Tbsp parsley, finely minced

1 Tbsp thyme leaves

Zest of 1 small lemon, finely minced

1 Tbsp smooth Dijon mustard

1 Tbsp kosher salt

Dusting of ground
  white pepper

1 Tbsp extra virgin olive oil

1 cup Madeira wine

Procedure

Loosen the meat from the ribcage to about ½ inch down from the end, leaving the meat attached to the bone. Mash together the garlic, chives, parsley, thyme leaves, lemon zest, and mustard to create a paste. Rub the mixture into the meat facing the bone. With two pieces of twine, fasten the meat back to the ribcage. Mix together the salt, pepper, and olive oil and rub it into the outside of the roast. Place the meat into a roasting pan, add the Madeira wine and cover with aluminum foil or a lid. Roast in a preheated 475-degree oven for 1 hour and 30 minutes. Reduce the heat to 400, uncover the roast and nicely brown it for about another 30 minutes.

For Dijon Mustard Sauce
Ingredients

Roasting juices

¼ cup Madeira wine

½ cup Demi-glace (pg. 21)

1 Tbsp crème fraîche (pg. 25)

1 tsp black truffle oil

1 Tbsp smooth Dijon Mustard

Procedure

To make the sauce, drain off roasting juices into a saucepan and degrease if needed. Add ¼ cup Madeira wine and place over high heat to reduce to one-half its volume. Add Demi-glace, crème fraîche, truffle oil, and mustard. Bring the sauce to a fast boil and serve it with the roast.

Swiss Meringue with Raspberry Chocolate Ice

YIELD: 4 servings

Ingredients

4 Swiss Meringue Nests (see below)

Raspberry Sorbet (see next page)

4 Tbsp single malt chocolate liqueur

Apple-Raspberry Sauce (pg. 29)

20 Fresh raspberries

8 Mint leaves

Fresh whipped cream (pg. 149)

Procedure

Place a 2-ounce ladle of Apple-Raspberry Sauce onto a dessert plate. It should fill the interior. Place a meringue nest in the middle of the sauce. Add a scoop of raspberry sorbet to the meringue and glaze the sorbet with the chocolate liqueur. Garnish with fresh raspberries, mint leaves, and fresh whipped cream.

Swiss Meringue Nests

YIELD: 20 servings

Ingredients

6 large egg whites

½ tsp crème of tartar

2 cups sifted vanilla sugar (pg. 150)

Procedure

A day ahead separate egg whites from yolks. Keep covered overnight at room temperature.

Preheat the oven to 200 degrees. Line a baking sheet with parchment paper and draw twenty 3-inch circles on it. Beat egg whites until frothy, then incorporate the crème of tartar. At medium speed, beat in 1 cup of the sugar and beat until soft peaks form. Mix in ½ cup more sugar. Increase speed to high and beat until stiff peaks form. Gradually incorporate the rest of the sugar and continue beating until meringue is stiff, glossy, and stands up. Fill a pastry bag, fitted with a small metal tip, with meringue and decoratively pipe out 20 nests. Nests should be about ¾-inch high. Bake the nests in the preheated oven for 3 hours. To "crisp" the nests, turn off the oven heat and let them cool in the oven for 1 hour with the oven door ajar.

When cool enough, nests can be brushed with dark melted chocolate for dessert purposes. Store nests between parchment paper in an airtight container at room temperature. They will keep indefinitely.

FAWN BROOK FAMILY MEMORIES

Homework

It may come as a surprise that a favorite memory has anything to do with homework. I was not the best of students, and as follows, was not really inclined to complete my studies. But thinking back on those times, how enjoyable it was to sit at a lantern-lit table next to a roaring fire, with classical music in the air on a cold winter's night. Mom's doctored hot cocoa may have helped some as well.

Raspberry Sorbet

YIELD: 6 cups

Ingredients

¾ cup water

¾ cup sugar

4 cups fresh raspberries

¼ cup orange vodka

¼ cup rose petal syrup (pg. 29)

1 Tbsp lemon extract

Procedure

In a saucepan, combine the water and sugar and boil for 10 minutes over high heat. Refrigerate to cool. In a food processor, puree the raspberries, orange vodka, and rose petal syrup. Add the cooled sugar syrup and the lemon extract. Transfer to a container and freeze for 1 hour and 30 minutes. It should have a slushy consistency. Pour into food processor again and puree. Return the mixture to the container and freeze for 3 to 4 hours.

DINNER THREE
GRILLED TENDERLOIN
OF VENISON "FORESTIERE"

APPETIZER: Applewood Smoked Salmon on
Garlic Toast Points (pg. 47) and Dill Sauce (pg. 26)
Pino Blanc from Austria 2002

SOUP: Beef Broth (pg. 51) with deep fried Spatzle (pg. 65)

SALAD: Romaine Lettuce with Star Fruit and Avocado
with Apricot-Lemon Vinaigrette (pg. 33)
Salted Breadsticks (pg. 146)

ENTRÉE: Grilled Tenderloin of Venison "Forestiere"
Served with a reduced game sauce of Port and Blueberries
accompanied with Vegetable Timbale,
Potato Croquets (pg. 76), and
sautéed Shiitake Mushrooms
Taltarni Shiraz 2001 from the Pyrenees Mountains of Australia

DESSERT: Salzburger Nockerln (pg. 163)
with Vanilla Sauce (pg. 148)
Spanish Coffee

Grilled Tenderloin of Venison "Forestiere"

YIELD: 4 servings

Ingredients

4 8-oz center cut venison tenderloin steaks

1 oz black truffle oil

Dusting of salt

Dusting of freshly ground white pepper

3 Tbsp garlic butter

2 Tbsp shallots, finely minced

1 Tbsp pink peppercorns, smashed

1 Tbsp sage leaves, coarsely chopped

8 large shiitake mushrooms, stems removed

1 oz Absolut Kurant vodka

1 recipe Game Sauce with blueberries (pg. 22)

Procedure

With a sharp knife, remove silver skin from the meat. Brush the steaks with the truffle oil and lightly dust with salt and pepper. Cover them with plastic wrap and let them marinate for about 2 hours. On a hot grill, brown the meat on all sides and grill them to medium rare. *Game meat can become quite tough if overcooked.* In a skillet, lightly glaze the shallots, pink peppercorns, and sage in the garlic butter. Add the mushrooms and sauté them just al dente. Add the grilled meat to the skillet and carefully flambe them with the Kurant vodka. Serve the hot game sauce on the side.

Viennese "Weinheber."

Vegetable Timbale

YIELD: 4 servings

Ingredients

2 small English cucumbers, 2 inches long

Dusting of salt

Sprinkle of lemon juice

1 Tbsp olive oil

16 baby carrots, small green tops still intact

1 tsp sugar

1 tsp freshly chopped dill or parsley for garnish

Procedure

With a potato peeler or fluter, flute the English cucumbers from end to end. Cut four 1-inch rounds out of them. Scrub out the inside, leaving just a little flesh. To keep them firm on the inside, season them with a dusting of salt and lemon juice. Sprinkle some olive oil over them, cover with plastic wrap, and marinate them for about 4 hours. Just before serving, lightly warm them in their own juices in a skillet. Season baby carrots, with small green tops still intact, with a little sugar, and steam them al dente. Place them inside the warm cucumber rounds and sprinkle them lightly with fresh chopped dill or parsley.

Spanish Coffee

YIELD: 1 serving

Ingredients

½ oz 151 rum

1½ oz Kahlua

1 cup coffee

Fresh whipped cream (pg. 149)

¼ tsp raspberry liqueur or Peter Heering

1 cherry

Procedure

Rim a Collins glass with sugar. Add rum and light it while tilting the glass. Roll the glass until the sugar on the rim bubbles. Add Kahlua and coffee to within 2 inches of the top. Garnish with whipped cream and float raspberry liqueur or Peter Heering on top. Garnish with a cherry.

DINNER FOUR

MEDALLIONS OF SPRING LAMB "CHEF STYLE"

APPETIZER: Lobster-Crabmeat Terrine (pg. 42)
with Saffron-infused Mayonnaise (pg. 25)
Kir Royale

SOUP: Cream of Asparagus (pg. 55)
with Fleurons (pg. 64)

SALAD: Salad Greens with Roquefort Cheese
and Lemon Oil Dressing (pg. 33)
Sourdough Bread with Butter

ENTRÉE: Medallions of Spring Lamb "Chef Style"
served with various hot and cold sauces for dipping,
Green Beans and Pine Nuts in a burned butter sauce,
Skillet Fried Potatoes
Chateau Neuf du Pape "Mont Redon" 2001

DESSERT: Schwarzwalder Kirsch Torte (pg. 156)
Coffee and *Grappa di Brunello*

Kir Royale

Procedure

In a champagne flute, place 1.2 oz raspberry liqueur. Fill with dry sparkling wine.

Medallions of Lamb "Chef Style"

YIELD: 4 servings

Ingredients

    28 oz lean boneless lamb loin, cut into 3 equal pieces

    Dusting of salt and pepper

    4 Tbsp garlic butter (pg. 30)

    2 Tbsp shallots, minced

    1 tsp fresh rosemary leaves

    1 oz 151 rum

Procedure

Dust lamb pieces with salt and pepper. In a skillet, melt the garlic butter. Bring to a bubbling point and glaze the shallots in it, add the lamb pieces and quickly brown to rare. Place skillet in a 450 degree oven and cook for 15 minutes (for medium rare). Season with the rosemary leaves and quickly and carefully flambé with the rum. Serve the sauces for dipping in individual containers:

    ½ cup Raspberry Mint Sauce (pg. 29)

    1 cup warm Sauce Béarnaise (pg. 27)

    ½ cup hot black truffle infused Demi-glace (pg. 21)

    1 cup marinated sundried cherries at room temperature (see below)

Marinated Sundried Cherries

YIELD: 4 servings

Ingredients

    1 cup firmly packed sundried cherries

    ½ cup pure maple syrup

    1 Tbsp lemon extract

    1 Tbsp Cointreau liqueur

    1 Tbsp fine orange zest

Procedure

Combine all ingredients in a saucepan and bring to boil. Remove from heat, pour into a container and refrigerate overnight. The longer the cherries marinate, the softer they will become.

Green Beans with Roasted Pine Nuts and Butter

YIELD: 4 servings

Ingredients

2 lb clean green beans

Dash of lemon juice

4 Tbsp pine nuts

1 Tbsp butter

Salt and pepper to taste

Procedure

Sprinkle cleaned beans with a few drops of lemon juice and steam them. Lightly brown the pine nuts in bubbling hot butter. Pour nuts and butter over the beans, toss to coat. Season with salt and pepper to taste.

Skillet Fried Potatoes

YIELD: 4 servings

Ingredients

2 lb potatoes, preferably Yukon gold

Cold water

½ cup grape seed oil

4 oz lean bacon, chopped

1 Tbsp garlic, finely minced

⅓ cup shallots, diced

½ Tbsp parsley, coarsely chopped

Salt and pepper to taste

Procedure

Peel and grate the potatoes and plunge them immediately into a bowl of lightly salted water to prevent discoloration. Drain and dry them out well with paper towels. In a skillet, brown the bacon in grape seed oil until crisp. Add the garlic and shallots and glaze them just lightly. Add the potatoes and crisp them over a high heat, approximately 8 minutes on each side. Mix in the parsley, salt and pepper to taste before carefully turning the potatoes over to crisp the other side. Place potatoes onto a serving dish and serve at once.

GRILLED BREAST OF PHEASANT
"FAWN BROOK INN"

APPETIZER: Escargots en Croûte or
Wood Mushrooms en Croûte (pg. 47)
Campari Cocktail

SOUP: Cold Cream of Apple-Blueberry (pg. 62)

SALAD: Salad Greens with
Balsamic Vinaigrette Dressing (pg. 33)
White Rolls and Garlic Oil

ENTRÉE: Grilled Breast of Pheasant "Fawn Brook Inn"
A young tender pheasant breast marinated overnight
in lavender honey and extra virgin olive oil, lightly grilled
and glazed with a Vanilla-Saffron Sauce accompanied
with Chestnut-Mandarin Orange Stuffing,
Steamed Green Asparagus Spears with Sauce Hollandaise
Tandem "Keefer Ranch" Pinot Noir 2003

DESSERT: Pear Belle Helene
Fresh Pears poached in stock syrup served in
Almond Tulip Cookie Cups with Vanilla Ice Cream
and Chocolate Rum Sauce
Late harvest Chardonnay 1997

Campari Cocktail

1½ oz Campari served over ice in a 12-oz glass with a dash of sweet Vermouth, Seven Up, and lemon twist.

Grilled Breast of Pheasant "Fawn Brook Inn"

YIELD: 4 servings

Ingredients

4 6-oz boneless pheasant breasts	1 Tbsp lavender flowers
Dusting of salt and pepper	1 Tbsp Madras curry powder
1 cup honey	1 recipe Vanilla-Saffron
1 cup extra virgin olive oil	sauce (pg. 24)

Procedure

Place the pheasant breasts in a glass pan and dust with salt and pepper. Pour the honey and olive oil over the breasts and sprinkle the lavender over them. Cover and refrigerate overnight. Remove the breasts from the marinade and place them on grill on medium heat and cook 12 minutes on each side, basting with the marinade. Be careful to not overcook the meat. It should be pink inside. Game birds dry out very fast and will taste like old paper if overcooked. Whisk the curry powder into the hot Vanilla-Saffron sauce and glaze the pheasants with it. Serve immediately.

Chestnut-Mandarin Orange Stuffing

YIELD: 4 servings

Ingredients

4 oz cleaned chestnuts	2 oz butter
⅓ cup pure maple syrup	1 whole egg
4 oz mandarin orange segments	¼ cup heavy cream
Zest of 1 lime	¼ tsp vanilla sugar (pg. 150)
6 slices stale white bread, crust removed	

Procedure

In a saucepan, combine chestnuts with pure maple syrup and bring to a boil. Reduce heat and simmer until the chestnuts are soft. Add the orange segments and lime zest. Generously butter each slice of bread and place them standing on edge in a 2-cup loaf pan. Whisk the egg, cream, and sugar together and pour over the bread. Spoon the chestnut-orange mixture over the top and let stand for four hours. Cover with foil and bake in a preheated oven at 475 degrees for 30 minutes. Remove the foil and bake another 15 minutes. Let it cool slightly and then remove from the pan. Reheat before serving.

Steamed Green Asparagus Spears

YIELD: 4 servings

Ingredients

16–20 asparagus spears

1 lemon

Sauce Hollandaise (pg. 27)

Procedure

Sprinkle the spears lightly with lemon juice and steam in lightly salted water until crisp and tender. Glaze the spears with Sauce Hollandaise before serving.

Pear Belle Helene

YIELD: 4 servings

Ingredients

4 ripe Bosc pears

2 cups Stock Syrup (see below)

4 Almond Tulip Cookie Cups (see next page)

Chocolate Rum Sauce (pg. 149)

Vanilla ice cream (pg. 177)

For garnish:

Fresh whipped cream (pg. 149)

Chocolate shavings

Mint leaves

Procedure

Core and peel the pears and poach in the stock syrup to al dente (a paring knife will reach the core with slight resistance). Remove from the syrup and cool. Place the cooled pears in the Almond Tulip Cookie Cups, and glaze with the Chocolate Rum Sauce. Add a couple of scoops of vanilla ice cream on the side. Garnish the pear with freshly whipped cream, chocolate shavings, and mint leaves.

Stock Syrup

YIELD: 2 cups

Ingredients

2 cups dry sparkling white wine

½ cup lemon juice

1 cup sugar

1 cinnamon stick

Procedure

Combine all the ingredients and bring to a boil. Reduce heat and simmer for about 20 minutes.

Almond Tulip Cookie Cups

YIELD: 16 cups

Ingredients

⅔ cup vanilla sugar (pg. 150)

½ cup all-purpose white flour

½ cup blanched almonds, finely ground

1 whole large egg, lightly beaten

2 large egg whites

2 tsp lemon extract

1 Tbsp water

2 oz unsalted butter, melted

Grape seed oil

6 4-inch squares of heavy aluminum foil

Procedure

Mix the sugar, flour, and ground almonds in a mixing bowl. In a separate bowl, beat the whole egg until frothy. Add to the flour mixture with a wooden spoon. Add the egg whites, lemon extract, and water. Stir in the cooled melted butter. The mixture should be slightly runny. Brush grape seed oil on a warmed baking sheet and create six cookies on the sheet by using approximately 1½ tsp of batter for each. Using the back of the wooden spoon, moving in a circular motion, flatten out the batter until it is about ¼ inch thick and 4 inches in diameter. Keep them well separated as they will spread during cooking. Bake in a preheated oven at 435 degrees for 8 minutes, rotate the pan, and bake for another 3 minutes or until they are lightly browned 1 inch around the edges.

While the batter is cooking, prepare the forms used to create the cups. Find 6 glass jars about 1½ inches in diameter. (Store-bought spice jars work the best or try Grandma's tiny straight tea cups.) When the cookies are done, quickly remove one with a wide spatula and place on a foil square, then drape it over a glass jar, molding the cookie to the desired shape. Continue for the other five cookies. The cookies cool quickly and become stiff. If this happens before you finish molding all of them, place them back in a hot oven for a few seconds to make them pliable again.

Once the cookies have cooled, they will become brittle. Carefully remove them from the glass jars and store in an airtight container. Do not refrigerate as the cookies will soften and lose their form. They can be individually wrapped and frozen. Defrost them unwrapped in a warm, moist-free place before use.

DINNER SIX
VEAL PAUPIETTES WITH SAUCE "MAISON"

APPETIZER: Lobster Remoulade (pg. 44)
Murphy Goode Fume Blanc Reserve

SOUP: Cream of Artichoke (pg. 57) with Fleurons (pg. 64)

SALAD: Mixed greens with Vinaigrette (pg. 32) and
Brioche with Extra Virgin Olive Oil (pg. 142)

ENTRÉE: Paupiettes of Veal "Maison"
Braised Belgium Endive in garlic butter
Baked Soufflé Potatoes (pg. 76)
Dry Creek Vineyard Cabernet Reserve

DESSERT: Apple Beignettes (pg. 151) and
Vanilla Sauce (pg. 148)
Coffee and *Calvados*

Paupiettes of Veal "Maison"

YIELD: 4 servings

Ingredients

8 3-oz veal filets (2 per person)

4 oz Duck Force Meat Stuffing (see next page)

24 baby langoustines (prawns)

Extra virgin olive oil

Dusting of flour

8 3-oz puff pastry (pg. 64)

Egg wash (pg. 3)

Sauce Maison (see next page)

Procedure

Carefully butterfly filets, keeping one edge of the meat intact, and flatten filets to about 4–5 inches. Place ½ oz of force meat stuffing and 3 langoustines in the center of each piece. Tightly roll up the meat, tucking in the sides to keep the stuffing from escaping. Secure the rolls with a toothpick. In a skillet, heat the olive oil. Lightly dust each paupiette with flour and quickly brown all sides to seal the meat. Remove from the skillet and let them cool for a few minutes on a platter.

On a lightly floured cutting board, cut out a 5 x 7-inch rectangle of the puff pastry for each paupiette. Using a small cookie cutter, cut out decorations from the leftover puff pastry for decoration. Remove all the toothpicks from the meat. Brush edges of pastry with water. Place a piece of meat in the center and roll the pastry around it, tucking in the ends to seal. Place on an oiled baking sheet, with seams down, at least 2 inches apart to allow the pastry to puff. Decorate with cutouts, brush with egg wash, and place in a preheated 450 degree oven. Rotate the baking sheet after 10 minutes to insure paupiettes are evenly golden brown on all sides.

Serve with Sauce Maison on the side.

Duck Force Meat Stuffing

YIELD: 4 oz

Ingredients

1 Tbsp extra virgin olive oil

½ Tbsp shallots, finely diced

½ Tbsp garlic, finely diced

½ Tbsp chives, chopped

½ oz white bread, crust removed, cubed

1 large egg yolk

2 Tbsp heavy cream

4 oz duck breast meat

¼ tsp fresh thyme leaves

Dusting of nutmeg

Dusting of white pepper

Pinch of kosher salt

½ tsp lavender flowers

Procedure

In a skillet, heat the olive oil and lightly sweat the shallots, garlic, and chives. Add the cubed bread and just lightly toast it on all sides. Transfer the mixture to a bowl and mix in the egg yolk and cream. Set aside. Chop the duck meat to a fine consistency. Add meat and all of the seasonings to the bread mixture. Check for correct seasoning and add more salt and pepper if needed. Let the mixture rest for an hour before using.

Sauce Maison

YIELD: 4 servings

Ingredients

1 cup Demi-glace (pg. 21)

1 Tbsp black truffle oil

¼ cup sweet Vermouth

¼ cup crème fraîche (pg. 25)

Procedure

Combine all the ingredients in a saucepan over high heat and bring to a boil. Reduce the heat and gently simmer for about 8 minutes. Serve on the side with the Paupiettes of Veal.

COOKING CLASSES

For those who love to cook, private cooking classes are available in the spring and fall with master chef Hermann Groicher, and are offered for up to eight people.

Snowshoeing and Chocolate Mousse weeks are also offered during the winter, which include lodging, cooking classes, guided snowshoeing, fine dining, massage, and hot tub relaxation. The week includes a fondue night with traditional Gruyère and Emmental cheese and a moonlight snowshoe outing that is followed up with dessert, hot-spiced wine, and hot chocolate. The grand finale is having the students prepare a seven-course gourmet meal.

Check The Fawn Brook Inn website for information: www.fawnbrookinn.com

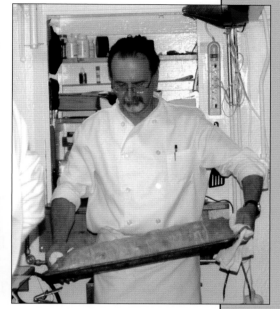

There's a log on the fire
The snow is falling
You're not getting any younger
What are you waiting for?

DINNER SEVEN

ROASTED DUCKLING WITH CHERRY-ORANGE SAUCE

Full Duck Dinner

APÉRITIF: Pernod Cocktail

APPETIZER: Smoked Trout Terrine (pg. 43) with
Roasted Pimiento–Ginger Sauce (pg. 26)
Grüner Veltiner White Wine

SOUP: Oxtail Soup (pg. 52)
with Cheese Puffs (pg. 66)

SALAD: Caesar (pg. 34)

ENTRÉE: Roasted Duckling with Cherry-Orange Sauce,
Potato Dumplings (pg. 74) and
Vegetable Mold in Aspic (pg. 72)
Cuvaison Merlot

DESSERT: Vanilla Ice Cream (pg. 177) with
Rose Petal Scented Syrup (pg. 29) served with
Single-Malt Whiskey Chocolate Sauce (pg. 149)
Coffee and *Cognac*

Pernod Cocktail

YIELD: 1 serving

Ingredients

3 oz Pernod

1 white sugar cube

Dash of cold water

Seedless lemon wedge

Procedure

Over a long 5-ounce champagne flute, place 2 toothpicks. On top of toothpicks, place a white sugar cube and slowly pour 3 ounces of Pernod over it. The sugar cube needs to dissolve as you pour the liquid over it. Finish the cocktail off with a dash of cold water. Remove the toothpicks and serve with a lemon wedge.

Roasted Ducklings

YIELD: 4 servings

Ingredients

4 oz carrots

4 oz celery

4 oz onion

4 oz leeks

4 oz turnips

2 young ducklings, weighing approximately 4 lbs each

2 sprigs of fresh rosemary

4 star anise

1 Tbsp whole cloves

4 oz orange

4 oz sliced lemon

1 Tbsp caraway seeds, whole

2 crumbled bay leaves

2 Tbsp English mustard powder

1 cup dry sherry

Salt and freshly ground white pepper to taste

½ oz mandarin orange liqueur

½ oz dark rum

Cherry-Orange Sauce (see next page)

Marinated Orange Zest (see next page)

Duck Sauce (see next page)

Procedure

Rinse the carrots, celery, onion, leeks, and turnips in cold water, then coarsely chop. Remove giblets, liver, and neck from the cavity of the ducklings. Rinse ducklings under cold water and pat dry. Place the rosemary sprigs, star anise, and cloves inside the cavity of each duck. Place chopped vegetables in a roasting pan and evenly distribute the sliced citrus fruits on top. Sprinkle the caraway seeds, bay leaves, and mustard powder over it. Pour the dry sherry inside the cavity of the ducks. Generously rub with salt and freshly ground white pepper before placing them in the roasting pan. Lightly prick the skin with a fork to release the fat while they are roasting.

Preheat oven to 450 degrees. Cover the pan with aluminum foil and roast for 2 hours. Carefully remove the foil and brown them for about 35–40 minutes or until they are nicely browned. Check for doneness by gently pulling on a leg. If the leg pulls away easily and there is no sign of blood in the juices, the ducks are done. Move the ducks to a cooling rack and let the fatty juices drip away. Normally the roasting juices are too fatty to be used for sauce.

(continued)

While the ducks are still warm, split them in half and cut away the backbone and carefully remove the ribcage and wishbone. Just before serving, place them on a tray and heat them in a hot oven. Remove from the oven and place them in a large skillet. Pour the mandarin liqueur and dark rum over the ducks and carefully flambé them.

To serve the ducklings, heat the Cherry-Orange Sauce and pour it over the ducks. Garnish with marinated orange zest and serve hot duck sauce on the side.

Cherry-Orange Sauce for Ducklings
YIELD: 4 servings
Ingredients

    4 oz sundried tart cherries

    2 Tbsp pure maple syrup

    2 Tbsp cherry brandy liqueur

    Marinated Orange Zest (see below)

Procedure
In a skillet over low heat, combine the cherries, syrup, and liqueur with the orange zest. Bring to a simmer, then let stand overnight.

Marinated Orange Zest
Ingredients

    Fine zest of one medium orange

    1 Tbsp orange liqueur

    1 Tbsp dark rum

Procedure
Marinate orange zest overnight in orange liqueur and dark rum.

Duck Sauce
Ingredients

    10 oz Demi-glace (pg. 21)

    2 Tbsp crème fraîche (pg. 25)

    ¼ cup tawny port

Procedure
Combine all the ingredients in a saucepan and bring to a boil. Reduce heat and gently simmer for approximately 10 minutes.

Breads

One must keep in mind that liquid forms are always measured in cups. Loose forms such as flour, ground nuts, etc., should always be measured by the ounce on a scale, as they are much lighter, and 1 cup is not necessarily a full 8 oz.

Crusty White Lemon Bread

YIELD: 2 1-lb loaves

Ingredients

1½ cups warm water (110 degrees)
1 Tbsp sourdough starter
2½ tsp active dry yeast
1 tsp sugar
2½ cups white all-purpose flour, divided, plus a dusting
1 Tbsp salt
1 Tbsp finely grated lemon zest
cooking spray for bowl
2 Tbsp lemon oil

Procedure

Place the warm water into a mixing bowl, stir in the starter and the yeast. Add the sugar and let it stand until the yeast starts to bubble up, approximately 15 minutes. With a dough hook, or by hand, mix in half the amount of flour and work it well. Add the salt, lemon zest, and remaining flour. Mix it until a smooth elastic dough is achieved. Add a dusting more of flour if needed. Place the dough on a lightly floured board and knead it 4–5 times with your hands, adding more flour if needed. Spray a large enough bowl with cooking spray. Form a smooth ball and place it into the sprayed bowl. Cover it with a warm towel and place it in a warm, draft-free place for about 45 minutes or until dough is doubled in bulk.

Again place dough on a lightly floured board, divide into 2 equal portions and work each into an 11-inch-long rope. Place ropes on a parchment-lined baking sheet, about 8 inches apart, as they double during proofing time. Make 3 diagonal slashes on each loaf with a sharp knife. Cover the loaves with a warm towel and proof them in a warm place until they double in size, about 30 minutes. Bake them in a preheated oven at 400 degrees for 45 minutes. Brush them generously with lemon oil and rotate the tray for even browning. Continue baking for 15 more minutes. Remove them from the oven and place them on a cooling rack.

NOTE: When baking bread in a dry atmosphere, it helps the proofing procedure if a pot of lightly boiling water sits on the stove. Also place a pan of hot water in the bottom of stove during baking procedure.

Butter Croissants

YIELD: 10 at 2½ oz each

Ingredients

¾ cup milk

¼ cup water

2 Tbsp active dry yeast

1 Tbsp sugar

½ tsp salt

1½ cups all-purpose white flour, divided, plus 1 cup for dusting

¼ lb butter at room temperature—butter needs to stay solid

A little melted butter

Procedure

In a saucepan bring milk and water to 110 degrees, then remove from heat. Dissolve yeast in it, add the sugar and salt and let it rest until yeast starts to work and bubble up, approximately 15 minutes. Slowly beat in 1½ cups of flour. Work it until dough is smooth and elastic. Place dough on a lightly floured board and work it well for about 8–10 minutes, adding a little flour at a time as needed. Place the dough into a well-greased bowl. Cover with a warm cloth and let it rest in a warm, draft-free place for about 1 hour or until doubled in bulk. Punch the sponge down and again rest it until doubled in bulk, about 30–45 minutes.

On a well-floured board, roll the dough out to a rectangle about 11 x 8 inches. Slice the butter into ¼-inch thickness and place slice by slice into the center of the dough. The butter should be warm, but still firm. Fold the ends of the dough over the butter from left to right, being sure ends are firmly sealed off. Carefully roll the dough out again to a rectangle of about 8 x 6 inches. Dust with flour as needed. Again, fold the dough out as first time. Repeat procedure two more times. Should any butter ooze out of dough, refrigerate until butter is well set and cold. Finish the rolling and folding procedure. Wrap the dough in plastic and refrigerate for about 45 minutes.

Roll the dough out to a circle of about 15 inches in diameter. Cut out 10 even pie-shaped wedges. Beginning at the circle edge, roll each one up tightly. Place them on a parchment paper-lined baking sheet. The points of the wedges need to be on the bottom. Keep them 2 inches apart and bend them into crescents. Again, cover with a cloth and proof them in a warm place for about 45 minutes. Bake them in a preheated oven at 400 degrees for 20 minutes. Lightly brush them with melted butter and bake them another 10–15 minutes or until they are nicely golden brown. Place them on a cooling rack right away.

See page 5 for tips on high-altitude baking.

Brioche with Extra Virgin Olive Oil

YIELD: 1 loaf, approximately 3 lb, or 10 individual pieces

Ingredients

1 cup water, heated to 110 degrees

2 Tbsp active dry yeast

1 Tbsp vanilla sugar (pg. 150)

¼ cup extra virgin olive oil

1 Tbsp kosher salt

Zest of 1 small orange and lemon

1 Tbsp rosewater

4 cups all-purpose white flour, plus a dusting more

2 extra large eggs at room temperature

1 well-beaten egg yolk

Extra olive oil and flour to brush bread basket and crust of bread

Procedure

Place hot water into mixing bowl fitted with a dough hook. Gently incorporate yeast and sugar. Let the mixture rest until yeast starts to bubble up, approximately 15 minutes. Mix in the olive oil, salt, lemon-orange zest, and rosewater. Slowly mix in the flour and mix until a smooth elastic dough forms. Mix in the eggs. Use a dusting more of flour if needed. Brush a bowl with olive oil. Place dough into it and cover with plastic wrap and a warm towel. Let the dough rest in a warm, draft-free place for about 8 hours.

Generously brush a bread basket with olive oil and dust with flour. Place a straight-shaped teacup in center of basket. Punch down the dough and form a rope about 20 inches long. Place the rope into the basket around the cup, firmly sealing off the two ends. Cover with a warm towel and set in a warm place to proof for about 1 hour or until doubled in bulk.

Line a baking sheet pan with parchment paper. Dust it with flour and carefully turn the basket over and place the proofed dough and teacup onto it. Remove the basket and you should still see the weave pattern. Brush with beaten egg yolk and bake in preheated oven at 375 degrees for 30 minutes. Rotate pan for even browning and bake for another 15 minutes. Generously brush the crust with olive oil and bake for another 5 minutes or until nicely golden brown. Remove from oven and place on cooling rack. Once it is cool, remove the tea cup.

NOTE: If properly refrigerated, brioche dough can be made several days ahead of baking time. However, it needs to be removed from the refrigerator at least 4 hours before baking time for proper proofing.

Blueberry Muffins

YIELD: 12 muffins

Ingredients

2½ cups all-purpose white flour

5 tsp double-acting baking powder

1 tsp salt

1 extra large egg

¼ cup vanilla sugar (pg. 150)

3 Tbsp butter, melted

1¼ cups whole milk

1½ cups fresh blueberries (or 1 cup frozen), cleaned and well drained

Procedure

Brush muffin pans with oil and dust with flour. In a bowl, combine flour, baking powder, and salt. In a separate bowl, beat the egg, sugar, and butter until creamy and thick. Slowly incorporate the milk. Replace beater with a dough hook and quickly incorporate the dry ingredients. Fold in the berries with a spatula. Fill prepared cups ⅔ full. Bake in preheated oven at 400 degrees for 25 to 30 minutes. Remove the muffins from cups as soon as they can be handled.

FAWN BROOK FAMILY MEMORIES

Wienerschnitzel

This is by far my dad's favorite meal to prepare. He gets a certain smile on his face when the order comes in and you can almost hear birds singing on this shoulder, just like in a Disney movie. Okay, my description of this event might be a bit skewed (or just flat out wrong!). Instead of a smile, you see a scowl deepen his brow and Flight of the Valkyries playing overhead instead of beautiful birds. Despite the hatred of this meal that envelopes my dad, for some reason, which he'll have to explain, he made this meal for my son Alex. It is now a tradition that whenever Alex and my parents are together, this is a meal that MUST be made. With careful supervision from Oma, Alex pounds the meat, dips it in the flour, egg, and bread-crumbs and helps fry it up . . . all with Opa in the background offering encouragement and praises for a job well done. (For those that know my father, you'll know this is the farthest thing from the truth!)

Christmas Fruit Bread

YIELD: 1 loaf, about 2¼ lbs

Ingredients

½ cup heavy cream

½ cup water

2 Tbsp Cointreau liqueur

2 Tbsp dark Stroh's rum

1 Tbsp vanilla sugar (pg. 150)

Pinch of kosher salt

2 Tbsp dry active yeast

2½ cups all-purpose white flour, divided

Extra dusting of white flour to form loaf

1 large egg yolk, at room temperature

⅓ cup toasted sliced almonds

1½ cups marinated dried fruits (see next page)

cooking spray

Sprinkling of anise seeds

1 whole star anise

2 Tbsp melted butter

Powdered sugar

Procedure

In a saucepan combine cream, water, Cointreau, and rum and heat to 110 degrees. Add sugar and salt and place into a warm mixing bowl. At low speed, add the yeast and combine it well. Turn off the motor and let the mixture rest until the yeast starts to work and bubbles up, approximately 15 minutes. With a plastic spatula, loosen all yeast from sides of bowl, being sure no cold draft occurs. Turn mixer to low speed and carefully mix in 2 cups of flour; combine it well. Add the egg yolk, toasted almonds, and mix in the fruit. Incorporate it well, then slowly add the rest of the flour. If needed, add a dusting more flour.

The dough should easily pull away from the sides of the bowl. Place the dough on a well-floured tabletop and punch it down several times. Spray a large enough bowl with cooking spray. Place dough into bowl and cover with a warm towel. Place it in a warm draft-free place. It's best placed next to a warm oven. In dry conditions, have a pot of gently simmering water next to it to help the proofing time. Let the dough rest for about 35–40 minutes.

(continued)

Remove dough from the bowl onto a well-floured tabletop and work it into a loaf. Cover it with a warm towel and let it rest for about 15 minutes. Spray a bread pan with cooking spray and sprinkle the bottom with anise seeds. Place the loaf into prepared pan, smoothing out sides and corners, and with a knife make a cross-like incision on top of loaf. Insert the star anise into the center of the cross. Again, place the loaf in a warm, draft-free place covered with a warm towel and proof it for 30 minutes.

Place the bread in a preheated oven and bake at 375 degrees for 45 minutes. Generously brush the loaf with melted butter. Increase oven temperature to 400 and bake for another 20 minutes. Remove the bread from the pan as quickly as possible to a cooling rack and generously dust the top with powdered sugar. Cool the loaf completely before wrapping and storing it away in the refrigerator. Flavor of the bread will greatly improve with aging up to 4 weeks. Heat bread in a warm oven before use.

Dried Fruit Mixture
Ingredients

   1½ cups dried fruits of apple, pear, peach, apricot, figs, dates,
      pitted prunes, pineapple, mango, cherries, and raisins
   Fine zest of ¼ lemon and ¼ orange
   ¼ tsp green cardamom seeds
   Dusting of ground cloves
   Dusting of cinnamon
   2 Tbsp Stroh's rum
   2 Tbsp Grand Marnier liqueur

Procedure

Coarsely chop dried fruits. Add the lemon-orange zest. Combine with all seasonings and liquids and place in an airtight container. Keep it in a cool, dark place or refrigerator for up to 3 weeks. Turn container upside down and shake it well once a week.

Salted Bread Sticks

YIELD: 8 3-oz breadsticks

Ingredients

1 cup water
¾ cup milk
1 Tbsp sugar
2 Tbsp active dry yeast
2½ cups white flour, divided
1 Tbsp lemon extract
1 Tbsp salt, plus some extra
Egg wash (pg. 3)

Procedure

In a saucepan add half the milk to the water and bring it to 110 degrees. Add the sugar and stir in the yeast. Let it rest until the yeast starts to bubble, approximately 15 minutes. Vigorously work in 1½ cups of the flour. Cover dough with a towel and let it rest in a warm, draft-free place for one hour. Keep the rest of the milk in a warm place. Pour the remaining milk onto the dough and work in the rest of the flour, being careful since not all the flour may be needed. A smooth elastic dough should be achieved. Add 1 tablespoon salt to it and work it in well. Place the dough into a well-greased bowl. Cover with a towel and again let it rest in a warm place for 30 minutes.

Punch dough down and again let it rest another 30 minutes. Again punch it down and rest it for another 20 minutes. On a lightly floured board, form the dough into a long rope. Divide into 8 equal parts, about 3 oz each. With a rolling pin roll them out to a round disk, about ½-inch thick. Lightly brush the edges with lukewarm water and tightly roll them up. They should be about 5 inches long. Close off the ends. Place them on a lightly oiled baking sheet about 1½ inches apart, as they will grow while proofing. Place the tray in a warm place, covered with a towel, for 30 minutes.

With a sharp knife, slash the sticks at an angle 3 times. Generously sprinkle each with salt and bake them in a preheated oven at 400 degrees for 15 minutes. Brush with egg wash and increase the heat to 450 and bake for another 10 minutes. Remove them from the oven and place onto a cooling rack. The sticks should be eaten when warm. They are an excellent partner with a bowl of hot soup and a cool beer.

Desserts

Sauces and Other Garnishes for Desserts

(use only mildly flavored brandies, such as grappa or vodka)

Orange Coffee Infused with Vodka —A Specialty of Provence

YIELD: 750 ml bottle
CURING TIME: 44 days

Ingredients

1 medium-sized orange,
    preferably organically grown
50 well-roasted coffee beans
1 bottle (750 ml) vodka
22 white sugar cubes
Glass jar with lid—do not use metal containers

Procedure

Wash the orange and wipe it dry. With a sharp utility knife, make 50 incisions into the orange and insert the coffee beans. Place the vodka into the container. Add the sugar cubes and immerse the orange into it. Seal the container. Store in a cool, dark place. Every day, turn the container upside down and shake it well until sugar is completely dissolved. Continue shaking the container 2–3 times a week during curing procedure. After 44 days, strain the liquid into a bottle and discard the orange. It is excellent used in game pâté to marinate the meat instead of cognac or port. May also be used as a shot poured over fresh berries with ice cream or over ice as an after dinner drink as a variation. The orange can also be spiked with whole cloves, cinnamon, or star anise and used as a complement to hot tea.

Vanilla Sauce

YIELD: 1½ cups

Ingredients

½ cup heavy cream
5 extra large egg yolks
2 Tbsp vanilla sugar (pg. 150)
2 Tbsp Amaretto liqueur

Procedure

In a saucepan, bring the cream to scalding point—do not boil it. In a bowl, whip egg yolks with the sugar until thick. Slowly incorporate the Amaretto and the cream. Mix well. Place bowl over a simmering water bath (bowl should not touch the water) and whisk in a steady motion until thick and custard like, scraping down sides of bowl frequently to prevent the cream from cooking and getting gritty.

Crème Anglaise

YIELD: approx. 2 cups

Ingredients

2 cups heavy cream
12 large egg yolks
8 oz vanilla sugar (pg. 150)
3 Tbsp lime juice

Procedure

Bring the cream to scalding point—do not boil. In a mixing bowl, combine egg yolks and sugar and whip until thick and creamy. Reduce speed and carefully add the cream and the lime juice. Place bowl over a hot, but not boiling, water bath and continuously whip the cream until well thickened (bowl should not touch the water). Adjust the heat as necessary—never let water boil. Cream needs to be completely cold before it is used.

Whipped Cream

YIELD: 2 cups

Ingredients

8 oz heavy cream

2 oz powdered sugar

½ oz Kirschwasser (cherry brandy)

Procedure

Place cream in mixing bowl. Add sugar and whip on high speed until stiff peaks form. Add Kirschwasser at very last minute and incorporate well.

Pastry Cream

YIELD: 1 9-inch tart

Ingredients

¾ cup heavy cream

1 large egg yolk or two small ones

2 Tbsp vanilla sugar (pg. 150)

1 Tbsp cornstarch

1 oz macadamia liqueur or liqueur of preference

Procedure

Because of the small quantity of ingredients, it is extremely important to have everything ready before starting the cream. Also, the water temperature should be kept at simmering point. If cream thickens too fast, it will become lumpy* and will not taste right.

Warm cream over a double boiler. In a bowl, combine egg yolk and sugar and whip until creamy. Slowly add cornstarch, whisking until well combined. Add to warm—not hot—cream and continue whisking until thick. Slowly add liqueur and continue whisking until the cream thickens up again. Refrigerate the cream for 24 hours before using.

*TO AVOID LUMPY CREAM, be sure sugar and eggs are mixed together well. Also be sure that water temperature remains at simmering point or eggs will scramble when added to a cream that's too hot.

Single-Malt Whiskey Chocolate Sauce

YIELD: 3 pints

Ingredients

½ cup corn syrup

¼ cup water

1 vanilla bean, seeds only

14 oz dark chocolate, shaved

14 oz sweetened condensed milk

1 cup half & half

1 cup heavy cream

12 oz single malt whiskey,

   plus 2 oz extra if not used right away

Procedure

Combine corn syrup, water, and vanilla seeds. Bring to boil. Reduce heat and add the chocolate. Stir until chocolate is melted. Place into mixing bowl and add condensed milk, half & half, and cream. Mix until well combined. Slowly whisk in 12 oz whiskey, then fill pint-sized glass jars. Refrigerate for 2 days before using. Bring to room temperature and stir well before using. Pour over ice cream, add to ice as a drink, or mix with hot cocoa.

If keeping sauce for a while before using, add additional whiskey to the top of each jar to preserve, then seal jars. Mix the extra whiskey in before serving.

Chocolate Rum Sauce Liqueur

Use the Whiskey Chocolate Sauce recipe above, and substitute the single malt whiskey with 10 ounces strong dark rum, such as Stroh's rum from Austria.

Caramel Lime Sauce

YIELD: 2 cups

Ingredients

¾ cup water

¼ cup lime juice

1 lb granulated super fine sugar

1 Tbsp crème fraîche (pg. 25)

Procedure

Combine water and lime juice and set it over low heat. Bring to boiling point just before using in recipe. Place sugar in a separate saucepan and set it over high heat. Stir sugar continuously with a wooden spoon. As it starts to melt, sugar should not come to a boil. Reduce heat as needed. A slow melting process should be achieved, being sure all lumps dissolve. As sugar turns to a light amber color, very slowly and carefully add the boiling water. Reduce heat as soon as mixture starts to boil over. Keep stirring until all sugar lumps dissolve. Keep the caramel at simmering point for about 20 minutes. The consistency of the caramel should coat the wooden spoon very lightly when held up in the air, and should be of a very light brown color. Remove caramel from the heat and stir in the crème fraîche until dissolved. Strain the liquid through a fine wire-mesh sieve. To make plain caramel, omit crème fraîche and lime juice.

FLAVORED SUGARS

Superfine sugar is used in all Aromatic Sugars. *Keep all sugars away from high heat sources and direct sunlight. Keep them in airtight containers.*

Vanilla Sugar

Ingredients

1 vanilla bean

1 lb sugar

Procedure

Split vanilla bean lengthwise, quarter it, and insert into sugar. Store and age the sugar in an airtight container for about 3 weeks. Vanilla bean can be re-used up to 6 times. Put used beans in iced tea or syrups before discarding them.

Cinnamon Sugar

Ingredients

3 cups vanilla sugar (see above)

½ cup ground Ceylon cinnamon

Procedure

Combine well.

Fundraiser lunch.

Apple Beignettes

YIELD: 4 servings

Ingredients

4 medium-sized apples, cored, and sliced ¾ inch thick

Fresh lemon juice

Hot frying oil, preferably grape seed or canola oil

Beer batter (see below)

Cinnamon sugar (pg.150)

Powdered sugar

Vanilla Sauce (pg. 150)

Procedure

Sprinkle the apple slices with lemon juice to prevent discoloring. Bring oil in deep fat fryer up to 350 degrees. Pass apple slices through beer batter, being sure they are well coated with the batter, and carefully drop them into hot fat. Brown them nicely on both sides. Place them on paper towels to drain off excess fat. Sprinkle them generously with cinnamon sugar and powdered sugar. Serve them hot with Vanilla Sauce.

NOTE: If no deep fat fryer is available, an electric Chinese wok is just as efficient, or a deep skillet will do the purpose as well. However, special caution is advised with a skillet. Hot oil will splatter and could cause burning of skin. Also, if an open flame such as a gas flame is used, it could be a fire hazard, so extra caution is advised.

Beer Batter

YIELD: 3 cups

Ingredients

8 oz all-purpose white flour

2 tsp active dry yeast

Dusting of nutmeg

Pinch of salt

4 Tbsp olive oil

1¼ cups beer

2 large whole eggs at room temperature

Procedure

Combine flour, yeast, nutmeg, and salt. Add the oil and beer, and mix it until well combined. Wrap it with plastic. Cover it with a warm towel and set it in a warm, draft-free place for 4 hours. After resting time, beat in the 2 warm eggs. Again cover it and let it rest for another 4 hours in a warm place before using. If batter is too thin, beat in extra flour.

Cherry Strudel
YIELD: 4–6 servings

Ingredients
1½ lbs puff pastry (pg. 64)

1½ lbs well-drained cottage cheese

1 lb pitted cherries, coarsely pureed

½ cup vanilla sugar (pg. 150)

3 Tbsp lemon extract

4 cups firmly packed pitted cherries

Dusting of cinnamon sugar (pg. 150)

2 cups toasted ground almonds

Cooking spray

Egg wash (pg. 3)

Mascarpone-Vanilla Sauce (see below)

Procedure
Roll puff pastry out to a rectangle of about 23 x 15 inches for strudel. Combine cottage cheese with pureed cherries, vanilla sugar, and lemon extract. Spread this mixture over the pastry, leaving about one inch free on all sides of dough. Evenly distribute the pitted cherries over the mixture. Generously dust the cherries with the cinnamon sugar and spread the ground almonds over it. Line a sheet pan with parchment paper and spray with cooking spray. Carefully and tightly roll up the strudel and place it on the parchment paper–lined sheet pan, being sure the seam of the strudel is to the bottom of the pan. Tuck in the ends, and with a fork, poke holes into the top for steam to escape during baking procedure. Brush with egg wash and bake in preheated oven at 475 degrees for 20 minutes. Rotate pan and bake for another 10 minutes or until strudel is nicely golden brown on all sides.

To Serve
Place warm strudel onto a pool of mascarpone vanilla sauce. Garnish with freshly whipped cream (pg. 149). Dust with cinnamon sugar (pg. 150) and powdered sugar.

Mascarpone-Vanilla Sauce
Ingredients
2 cups Vanilla Sauce (pg. 148)

½ cup mascarpone

Procedure
Mix and serve. Do not heat.

Apple Strudel

YIELD: 4–6 servings

Ingredients

2 tart apples, about 10 oz

Zest and juice of 1 small lemon

Dusting of white flour

11 oz puff pastry (pg. 64)

Grape seed oil or melted butter

⅓ cup ground pecans

⅓ cup breadcrumbs

2 oz vanilla sugar (pg. 150)

1 tsp ground cinnamon

⅓ cup golden raisins

⅓ cup currants

⅓ cup lightly toasted sliced almonds

1 whole egg, beaten well

Procedure

Core and slice apples. Sprinkle with lemon juice and zest to prevent discoloring. On a smooth surface, place a strong tablecloth, about 20 x 24 inches, being sure no seams or folds are in the cloth. Dust it lightly with the flour and roll the puff pastry out to about 12 x 8 inches. Brush the pastry with the oil or butter and evenly distribute the ground pecans, followed by the breadcrumbs. Drain the apples of excess lemon juice and place them evenly over the breadcrumbs. Sprinkle the sugar and the cinnamon over it. Evenly distribute the raisins, currants, and toasted almonds. With both hands, take hold of one end of the cloth. Gently lift the cloth, never touching the dough, to roll the strudel, jelly-roll style, away from you, being sure seam of strudel ends up on the bottom. Double line a baking sheet pan with parchment paper. Lift the strudel onto it, again being sure that the seam is on the bottom. Tuck in all ingredients that may have fallen out of the sides during this procedure, and seal sides tightly. Generously brush the strudel with the well-beaten egg and place in a preheated oven at 450 degrees and bake for 20 minutes. Reverse the pan, increase the temperature to 475, and bake for another 15 minutes or until strudel is nicely golden brown on all sides.

To Serve

Place strudel portion on a pool of vanilla sauce (pg. 148). Generously garnish with freshly whipped cream (pg. 149) and dust with cinnamon sugar (pg. 150) and powdered sugar.

Viennese Doughnuts

YIELD: 14 doughnuts

Ingredients

1 cup dairy cream

2 oz unsalted butter

3 cups all-purpose white flour, divided

Pinch of kosher salt

1½ Tbsp vanilla sugar (pg. 150)

Zest of 1 large lemon

1 Tbsp active dry yeast

5 extra large egg yolks

1½ Tbsp dark rum

1 tsp powdered sugar

1 large egg white

14 tsp apricot, orange,
  or raspberry marmalade

6 cups hot frying oil

Dusting of powdered sugar

Procedure

Place cream and butter in a saucepan and bring to scalding point. Do not boil it. Remove from heat and cool down to 105 degrees. In a bowl, combine 2 cups of flour, salt, sugar, lemon zest, and yeast. Slowly add cooled cream and mix with a wooden spoon. As soon as all the ingredients are well combined, beat the dough for about 5 minutes. Cover the dough with a warm towel without removing the wooden spoon. Set it in a warm, draft-free place and let it rise until double in volume, approximately 1½ hours.

Place egg yolks into a bowl. Add the rum and set the mixture over a simmering water bath, never letting the bowl touch the water, and beat with a whisk until lightly thickened. Remove from heat and continue whisking until lightly cooled. In a separate bowl, add powdered sugar to egg whites and beat until stiff peaks form. Carefully fold this into the cooled egg mixture. With a wooden spoon, slowly beat egg mixture into risen dough. When well combined, add the rest of the flour under constant beating. Stop adding flour as soon as the dough forms and loosens easily from sides of the bowl. Take dough in both hands and slap it vigorously from one hand to the other 4 to 5 times. Place the dough back in the bowl. Cover loosely and again let it rise in a warm place for about 30 minutes.

Generously dust a warmed cutting board with flour. Take dough into both hands and again form a smooth ball. Place on floured board and roll it out evenly, about ⅓-inch thick. With a 3-inch round cutter, cut out fourteen circles and place them on a parchment paper–covered sheet pan. Remove the rest of the dough from the board and again form it into a ball. Dust the board with flour if needed and let the dough rest on it. Place 1 teaspoon of marmalade on each cut-out circle. Roll out the remaining dough to ⅓-inch thickness and again cut out fourteen 3-inch circles. Moisten them lightly with warm water and place them on top of marmalade-filled circles, lightly pressing the edges together to seal them. With the tip of your thumb, gently press down the center of each doughnut, then cover them with a light cotton cloth and set in a warm, moist place. Let them rest for 30 minutes. They need to feel light and fluffy to the touch. Repeat the thumb procedure every 10 minutes.

In a deep fat fryer or an electric Chinese wok, heat grape seed oil or canola oil to 325 degrees. Place 3 doughnuts into it and brown them to a light golden color. With a slotted spoon, carefully turn them over and repeat the browning procedure. Remove the doughnuts quickly to a cooling rack lined with parchment paper and generously dust them with powdered sugar.

Hazelnut Cheesecake

YIELD: 12 servings

Needed

9-inch Teflon coated springform pan

Ingredients for Crust

4 oz softened unsalted butter

4 oz vanilla sugar (pg. 150)

3 large egg yolks

4 oz sifted all-purpose white flour

8 oz toasted hazelnuts, finely ground

Zest of 1 small lemon

Procedure

In mixing bowl, combine softened butter and vanilla sugar. Mix until creamy. Add egg yolks and mix well. In a separate bowl, combine flour and hazelnuts and slowly add to mixture. Beat until well combined. With plastic spatula, beat in lemon zest. Place mixture in refrigerator for about three minutes—just long enough for the dough to stiffen up a little. Wet fingers just a little with warm water and line coated springform pan, sides and bottom, with the dough. (If a plain metal springform pan is used, grease pan well with melted butter and dust with sifted white flour.)

Ingredients for Filling

3 whole large eggs

5 large egg yolks

½ cup fine granulated sugar

1½ lbs softened cream cheese, cut into small chunks

½ cup Frangelico liqueur

Ingredients for Topping

Juice of 1 small lime

1 cup crème fraîche (pg. 25)

Procedure

Combine eggs, egg yolks, and sugar in mixing bowl and whip until thick and creamy. Reduce speed and piece by piece add cream cheese. Mix until well combined, as cream cheese must be dissolved. Slowly add liqueur and combine well. Pour mixture into springform pan and bake cheesecake in preheated oven at 375 degrees for one hour. Before removing from oven, check for doneness. The top should be firm to the touch. Carefully insert a clean toothpick or metal skewer. If it comes out clean, the cake is done. Bake a little longer if needed. Remove from oven and cool on a wire rack for about 15 minutes. Combine lime juice and crème fraîche and gently pour it over the cake. Refrigerate for at least 8 hours before cutting the cake. The cheesecake must be totally cooled before removing from the springform pan.

Hot Spiced Wine

YIELD: 4 servings

Ingredients

13 oz red wine,
   Cabernet or Pinot Noir
13 oz white wine,
   Sauvignon Blanc
5 oz vanilla sugar (pg. 150)
¼ cup dark rum
2 star anise
2 bay leaves
5 cloves
½ medium lemon
½ medium orange
4-inch cinnamon stick

Procedure

In a saucepan combine wines with sugar and seasonings. Lightly squeeze in the juice of the lemon and orange, then add the lemon and orange rinds. Bring to the boiling point, but do not boil! Lightly simmer for 10 to 15 minutes. Drain the liquid through a wire-mesh sieve, and discard seasonings and fruits. Serve wine hot with a cinnamon stick and a slice of orange.

Black Forest Cherry Torte (Schwarzwalder Kirsch Torte)

All ingredients for this torte should be done 1 day ahead—the cake bases, the chocolate mousse, and the cherries.

YIELD: 2 9-inch torte bases; 12–14 servings

Ingredients

5 oz dark chocolate, melted
2 large whole eggs
8 large egg yolks
⅓ cup vanilla sugar (pg. 150), divided
8 large egg whites
1 oz Kirschwasser (cherry brandy)
1 tsp baking powder
4 Tbsp ground arrowroot
⅓ cup cacao powder
1 cup toasted hazelnuts, ground

Procedure

Spray two 9-inch cake pans with a good quality cooking spray. Over a simmering double boiler melt the chocolate and set it aside. In a mixing bowl, combine whole eggs and egg yolks. Add half the amount of vanilla sugar and at high speed mix until thick. In a separate bowl, beat egg whites until soft peaks form. Slowly incorporate the rest of the sugar to them and set aside. As soon as egg yolk mixture thickens, reduce the speed and add the Kirschwasser, the baking powder, arrowroot and cacao. Carefully beat in the egg whites—do not over-mix the batter. With a spatula, fold in the cooled melted chocolate and the ground hazelnuts. Place the batter into the cake pans and smooth the tops. Place them on a baking sheet and bake in preheated oven at 375 degrees for 30 minutes. Rotate the tray and bake for another 15 minutes. If done, bases should easily pull away from sides of the pan. Remove the cakes from the pans as soon as they can be handled. Place them on a cooling rack. Refrigerate for a couple of hours before assembling the torte.

Cherry Filling
Ingredients

1 lb pitted bing cherries, fresh or frozen—
   do not use canned cherries as they easily turn to mush
1 cup stock syrup (see below)

Stock Syrup
Ingredients

1 cup dry sparkling wine
¼ cup cherry liqueur
2 Tbsp lemon extract
½ cup sugar
¼ vanilla bean, chopped
1 2-inch long cinnamon stick
7 whole cloves

Procedure

In a saucepan, combine wine, liqueur, and lemon extract. Add the sugar and vanilla bean and all other spices. Bring to a boil. Reduce the heat and simmer the syrup for about 20 minutes or until reduced to about 1 cup. Strain and pour over the cherries. Refrigerate for at least 1 day before use.

Assembly of Black Forest Torte
Ingredients

- 1 recipe Cherry Filling
- 2 9-inch torte bases
- 2 recipes Chocolate Mousse (pg. 173)

Procedure

Drain the marinated cherries well and reserve the juice. Reserve 12–14 cherries for garnish. Spread the top of the bottom cake base with chocolate mousse. Use a dry metal spatula for this purpose as a spatula dipped in water will liquefy the mousse. Drain cherries of liquid before placing on cake. Place the cherries in a ring form pattern keeping the cherries as close together as possible. Lightly coat them with more mousse. Place the second cake base on top, gently pressing it down. Spread the rest of the mousse all around the torte, plus on top if any is left. Refrigerate the torte for a couple of hours to let the mousse get firm.

Garnish
Ingredients

- 1 quart heavy cream
- 2 Tbsp powdered sugar
- 1 Tbsp Kirschwasser
- 12–14 cherries reserved from Cherry Sauce
- ~3 oz shaved dark chocolate
- 1 cup Apple Glace (pg. 29)
- Juice from drained marinated cherries

Procedure

Whip the cream with the sugar until stiff peaks form. At the last minute, incorporate the Kirschwasser. Fill a pastry bag with the cream, fitted with a star tip, and decorate the entire torte with it. Evenly place 12–14 cream rosettes on the outer edges of the torte and fit the cherries into them. Cover the entire torte with the chocolate shavings. Combine the apple glace with the cherry juice and reduce to a light glace over medium heat. Place a pool of the glace on each serving plate and serve torte slices on it.

Sacher Torte

YIELD: 2 9-inch bases; 10–12 servings

Ingredients

5 oz dark chocolate melted

2 large whole eggs

8 large egg yolks

⅓ cup vanilla sugar (pg. 150), divided

8 large egg whites

1 oz dark rum

1 tsp baking powder

4 Tbsp ground arrowroot

⅓ cup cacao powder

1 cup toasted almonds, ground

2 cups Apricot Glace (see below)

~2 cups Chocolate Glace (see next page)

Procedure

Follow the procedure as outlined for Black Forest Cherry Torte (pg. 156). Replace Kirschwasser with rum, and hazelnuts with almonds.

Apricot Glace

YIELD: 2 cups

Ingredients

1 cup water

1 Tbsp lemon extract

1 cup vanilla sugar (pg. 150)

6 oz dried chopped apricots

½ cup apricot liqueur

1 Tbsp rose petal syrup (pg. 29)

Procedure

Combine water and lemon extract and bring it to a boil. Reduce the heat; keep the water gently simmering. Place sugar in a saucepan. Set it over high heat and stir continuously with a wooden spoon. Melt the sugar until a light amber color is achieved. Reduce the heat and very carefully and slowly add the simmering water to it. Keep stirring the caramel until all sugar lumps are dissolved. Adjusting the heat source, insert a candy thermometer and bring the caramel to 200 degrees. Carefully add the chopped apricots, the liqueur, and the rose syrup and bring it back to 200 degrees. Gently simmer it for about 8 minutes. Remove from the heat source and cool the mixture for 30 minutes. Place the cooled mixture into a food processor and puree the glace to a smooth consistency.

Chocolate Glace

YIELD: approximately 2 cups

Ingredients

8 oz dark semisweet chocolate, shaved

1 cup water

1 cup super fine sugar

1 oz dark rum

1 Tbsp extra virgin olive oil

Procedure

Over a simmering double boiler, slowly melt the chocolate. Turn off the heat as soon as chocolate is melted. In a saucepan, combine water and sugar. Set over heat and keep stirring until all sugar is dissolved. Insert a candy thermometer into liquid and bring it up to 220 degrees. Immediately remove from heat and carefully stir it into the melted warm chocolate. Combine it well then slowly mix in the rum and the olive oil, again mixing all ingredients well. Set aside to cool.

Assembly of the Sacher Torte

With a hot wet metal spatula, coat the top of the first torte base with ⅓ of the apricot glace. Spread a fine layer of chocolate glace on second base and sandwich the two bases—chocolate and apricot glace—together. Cover entire torte with the rest of the apricot glace. Refrigerate it for about 1 hour until apricot glace is well set. Again, with a hot wet metal spatula, glaze the whole torte with the chocolate glace. Again refrigerate the torte until chocolate glace is hardened. Cut the torte into 10 to 12 wedges. Use a wet hot knife for this purpose. Serve the torte with a generous dusting of powdered sugar and plenty of freshly whipped cream (pg. 149).

Bûche de Noël (Yule Log)

YIELD: 1 roll, 12 inches long, 12 servings

Ingredients

6 large egg whites

2 oz softened butter

6 oz vanilla sugar (pg. 150)

8 large egg yolks

2 oz dark rum

6 oz blanched almonds, finely ground

2 oz white flour

Grape seed oil

White Chocolate Filling (see below)

Dark Chocolate Outside Glace (see next page)

Chopped pistachio nuts for garnish

Powdered sugar for garnish

Meringue Mushrooms (see next page)

Procedure

In a bowl, whip egg whites until peaks form, and set aside. In a separate bowl, combine softened butter and sugar and whip until thick and creamy. Add egg yolks to it one at a time. Add rum. Keep whipping the mixture until well combined. Carefully mix in the almonds and flour and fold in the stiffly beaten egg whites. Line a jelly roll pan with double folded parchment paper and brush the paper and sides of pan with the grape seed oil. Evenly distribute the batter and bake in preheated oven at 400 degrees for about 15 minutes. On a level worktable, place a 16 x 24-inch piece of parchment paper. Brush it well with oil and gently tip the finished cake onto it. Just slightly cool the cake for about a minute and evenly spread the white chocolate filling over it. Tightly and carefully roll it up, being sure the ends are filled and smooth. Fit a pastry bag with a star tip and cover the log lengthwise with the dark chocolate outside glace, making it look like rough bark on a pine tree. Sprinkle entire log with coarsely chopped pistachio nuts and powdered sugar. Decorate with meringue mushrooms.

White Chocolate Filling for Yule Log

YIELD: for one log

Ingredients

4 oz very soft unsalted butter

6 oz vanilla sauce (pg. 148), flavored with 1 oz raspberry liqueur

5 oz white chocolate, melted, slightly cooled

Procedure

Whip the softened butter until creamy and slowly incorporate the vanilla sauce. Carefully fold in the melted chocolate.

Dark Chocolate Outside Glace for Yule Log

YIELD: for one log

Ingredients

4 oz softened butter

6 oz Crème Anglaise (pg. 148), flavored with 1 oz dark rum

6 oz dark chocolate, melted and slightly cooled

Procedure

Whip the softened butter until creamy and slowly incorporate the crème anglaise. Carefully fold in the melted chocolate.

Meringue Mushrooms

YIELD: about 20 2-inch mushrooms

Ingredients

2 large egg whites

¼ tsp crème of tartar

½ cup + 1 Tbsp superfine sugar

Dusting of cocoa powder

Dusting of powdered sugar

Procedure

A day ahead, separate egg whites from yolks. Keep covered overnight at room temperature. Preheat oven to 200 degrees. Line a baking sheet pan with parchment paper. Beat egg whites until frothy. At medium speed, mix in the crème of tartar. Add 2 Tbsp of the sugar and beat until soft peaks form. Add 1 Tbsp of the sugar and increase speed to high. Beat until stiff peaks form. Gradually beat in the remaining sugar and continue beating until meringue is stiff, glossy and stands up.

Fill a pastry bag, fitted with a #3 round decorating tip, with meringue and pipe out the mushroom tops—about 2 inches in diameter at the base. Round them out to a dome shape. Keep the tip of the metal tube buried in the meringue for best effect and release pressure as you bring the tip to the surface.

To pipe out the stems, hold the pastry bag upright with the tube touching the baking sheet. With pressure, keep the tip buried in the meringue as you build up a cone about ¾ inches high. Keep the bases wider than the top ends so they don't topple over. Save a little of the meringue to finish the mushrooms. Place the meringues in the preheated oven for 3 hours or until they are firm and dry to the touch.

To finish the mushrooms, poke a small hole on the bottom of the mushroom cup with the tip of the metal tube. Apply a dash of meringue and insert the stem into the cup. Let them dry for 1 hour. Lightly dust the mushrooms with cocoa powder and powdered sugar. Store mushrooms in an airtight container at room temperature. They will keep indefinitely.

Dobos Torte

YIELD: 6 discs—1 torte

Ingredients

10 large egg yolks

10 oz vanilla sugar (pg. 150), divided

2 Tbsp lemon extract

Zest of 1 lemon

10 large egg whites

7 oz blanched almonds, finely ground

2 oz white cake flour

Chocolate Butter Cream (see below)

Caramel Sauce (see below)

Procedure

Lightly spray six 9-inch cake pans on the sides and bottom with cooking spary. Place 6 round parchment paper circles on bottom of pans. Combine egg yolks and 8 oz of vanilla sugar and whip at high speed until eggs turn creamy and thick. Add the lemon extract, lemon zest, and incorporate well. In a separate bowl, add 2 ounces of vanilla sugar to the egg whites and whip them until peaks form, and set aside. Slowly add the ground almonds to egg batter and incorporate well, then add the flour and mix well. With a plastic spatula, carefully fold in the egg whites until well incorporated. Place equal amounts of batter into prepared cake pans, smooth out the tops and bake the discs in preheated oven at 350 degrees for 30 minutes, or until the sides pull away easily from the cake pans. Carefully remove the disks and place onto a parchment paper-lined cooling rack.

Chocolate Butter Cream
Ingredients

4 oz dark chocolate, melted

1 oz apricot liqueur

½ cup Apricot Glace (pg. 158)

12 oz softened butter

2 cups Crème Anglaise (pg. 148)

Procedure

Over a simmering double boiler, slowly melt the chocolate and set aside. In a bowl, incorporate apricot liqueur with the apricot glace. In a separate bowl, whip the softened butter until very creamy, then incorporate the crème anglaise. Add the apricot glace and mix well. With a plastic spatula, carefully fold in the melted chocolate, being sure chocolate is somewhat cooled down so as not to melt the butter cream. Refrigerate the cream just long enough to stiffen up a little.

Caramel Sauce
Ingredients

1 lb superfine sugar

¼ cup lime juice

Procedure

Melt the sugar completely until an amber color is achieved. Carefully add the lime juice. Continue to simmer the caramel until liquid is evaporated. Keep it warm until ready to use.

Assembly of Dobos Torte

Sandwich together 5 disks with the chocolate butter cream. Smooth out the sides and top. Decorate the top with 6 butter cream spirals. Coat the last disk generously with the caramel and with a sharp, wet knife, cut 6 equal slices. Let the caramel harden. Place the slices in a somewhat slanted position on the butter cream spirals as a final decorative finishing touch.

Salzburger Nockerln

YIELD: 4 servings

Ingredients

⅓ cup milk

2 oz butter

5 large egg yolks

4 oz vanilla sugar (pg. 150), divided

5 large egg whites

2 Tbsp white flour

Powdered sugar for dusting

1 cup Vanilla Sauce (pg. 148)

Procedure

Scald the milk and pour into soufflé dish. In a bowl, combine butter, egg yolks, and half the sugar, and beat until creamy and thick. In a separate bowl, beat the egg whites until very stiff. Slowly add the rest of the sugar to the egg whites. Carefully stir the flour into the egg yolk mixture, then fold the whites into the yolk mixture. Don't over-mix. Pour mixture into dish with the scalded milk and place into preheated hot oven. Bake at 425 degrees until top is nicely browned, about 25 minutes. Generously dust the top with powdered sugar and quickly serve with vanilla sauce.

NOTE: This is a basic recipe for any hot soufflé. Keep in mind that all flavorings and liquids need to be mixed in with the egg yolk mixture.

Apple-Apricot Ginger Cake

YIELD: 1 9-inch springform pan

Ingredients

¼ lb. unsalted butter, softened

½ cup vanilla sugar (pg. 150)

3 large whole eggs

1 cup white flour

1 tsp. baking powder

pinch of salt

Marinated Fruit (see below)

1 cup warm apricot preserves

sprinkle of sliced toasted almonds

Fresh whipped cream (pg. 149)

Procedure

Spray the springform pan with cooking spray. In a mixing bowl combine softened butter and vanilla sugar and beat until creamy and fluffy. Beat in whole eggs one at a time until well combined. In a separate bowl, combine flour, baking powder, and salt. Slowly incorporate into egg batter mixture. Fold in the marinated fruit mixture including excess juices, combine well and pour into prepared springform pan. Bake the cake in preheated oven at 375 degrees for 45–50 minutes. Remove cake from oven and place on cooling rack. Remove springform and glace the cake with the warm apricot preserve, sprinkle the toasted almonds on top, and serve with freshly whipped cream.

Marinated Fruit
Ingredients

Zest of ½ medium lemon

Zest of ½ medium orange

3 Tbsp lemon juice

3 Tbsp orange juice

¼ cup Grand Marnier liqueur

3 apples, cored and sliced (28 oz)

6 oz juliennes of dried apricots

3 oz golden raisins

3 oz crystallized ginger

dusting of cinnamon and sugar

Procedure

Combine above ingredients and refrigerate for 24 hours.

PIES AND TARTS

Pie or Tart Shell with Nuts

YIELD: 1 9-inch pie or tart shell

Use almonds, macadamias, pecans, hazelnuts, etc. Nuts need to be lightly toasted and finely ground, preferably in a nut mill. If a food processor is used, proceed slowly and with caution. Because of a high oil content in nuts, mixture can turn to a paste in seconds.

Ingredients

2½ oz unsalted butter at room temperature

2 oz vanilla sugar (pg. 150)

4 oz finely ground nuts

4 oz all-purpose white flour

1 Tbsp lemon extract

½ Tbsp lemon zest

Procedure

Combine softened butter and sugar and beat until fluffy. Slowly add the nuts and the flour. Combine well. Beat in the lemon extract and lemon zest. Wrap the dough in plastic wrap and refrigerate for about 30 minutes to stiffen up. Lightly spray tart or pie tin with cooking spray. With your fingertips, press in the dough to the sides and bottom of the tin, extending the dough about ⅓ inch above sides of the tin. Bake in preheated oven at 375 degrees; for a prebaked pie shell, 30 minutes; for tarts, about 45 minutes.

NOTE: Since no eggs are used in this recipe, beans, rice, or metal pellets are not needed. When prebaking the shell, it will keep its form perfectly well.

Pie Pastry Shell

YIELD: 1 9-inch pie shell

Ingredients

2 oz unsalted butter or lard

3 oz all-purpose white flour

½ tsp kosher salt

2 Tbsp cold milk

Procedure

Bring butter or lard to room temperature. Combine flour and salt in mixing bowl. Cut in the butter or lard with a pastry blender or with two knives, and work it until the mixture is the consistency of coarse cornmeal. Slowly incorporate the milk. Start mixing the dough with a fork and work it until a smooth, elastic dough is achieved. If dough is sticky, work in just a dusting of flour. Form to a smooth ball. Dust a smooth tabletop lightly with flour and with a rolling pin roll the dough out to an 11-inch circle. The circle should be ⅛-inch thick.

Lightly spray 9-inch pie pan with cooking spray. Fold the rolled dough in half and ease it loosely into pie pan with the fold in the center. Carefully unfold the dough and fit it into the pan. Gently press dough into pan so no air pockets remain. Flute the edge of pie pan if so desired. If the shell needs to be prebaked, prick the bottom with a fork and prebake at 475 degrees for about 20 minutes or until the shell has a light golden hue. If a top crust is called for, simply double the recipe; however, do not roll out the top crust at the same time. Roll out top crust when pie is ready to be finished.

Brown Sugar

To keep brown sugar from getting hard once the package is opened, add 2 or 3 slices of apples or a small slice of bread and store in an airtight container.

Coconut Pastry Shell

YIELD: 1 9-inch pie shell

Ingredients

¼ cup unsalted butter
  at room temperature

¼ cup vanilla sugar (pg. 150)

3 oz dry unsweetened
  coconut flakes

½ tsp lemon zest

2 oz sifted all-purpose white flour

1 Tbsp dark rum

Procedure

In a mixing bowl, combine butter and vanilla sugar with a fork until fluffy. Add the coconut, lemon zest, and flour. Work it until a smooth dough is achieved. Incorporate the rum and work dough into a smooth ball. Double wrap the ball in plastic and refrigerate it for 1 hour. Lightly spray a pie pan with cooking spray. Press dough evenly into pie pan extending it just about ⅛-inch above the rim of the pie pan. Flute the overhang according to desired thickness. Set aside until ready for filling.

Apple Pumpkin Pie

Yield: 1 9-inch pie

Ingredients

Coconut pie shell, unbaked (above)

3 medium-sized granny smith
  apples (about 3 cups)

Lemon juice

2 Tbsp unsalted butter

½ cup brown sugar

½ cup dark rum

1 Tbsp arrowroot

1 tsp ground cinnamon

Pinch of kosher salt

1 cup pumpkin pulp, solidly packed

1 cup mascarpone

⅓ cup condensed milk

1 Tbsp vanilla sugar (pg. 150)

1 tsp ground ginger

1 whole large egg, well beaten

Fresh whipped cream (pg. 149)

Dusting of powdered sugar

Procedure

Prepare the coconut pie shell. Peel and slice the apples, sprinkle with lemon juice to prevent discoloring, and set aside. In a large enough saucepan, combine butter, brown sugar, dark rum, arrowroot, cinnamon, and salt. With constant stirring, cook over high heat until a caramelized consistency is achieved. Quickly add sliced apples. Coat them well with the syrup. Reduce the heat and gently simmer to al dente.

Fill pie shell with the apple mixture. Combine pumpkin pulp, mascarpone, condensed milk, vanilla sugar, ginger, and well-beaten egg. Pour mixture over the apples. Smooth them out and bake the pie in preheated oven at 375 degrees for about 1 hour. Check for doneness with a toothpick. To prevent the edges from getting too dark, cover edges with foil. Refrigerate until cold. Before cutting the pie, decorate with swirls of fresh whipped cream and a dusting of powdered sugar.

Apple Almond Pie

YIELD: 1 9-inch pie

Ingredients

5 medium-sized firm apples (about 1½ lb)

1 Tbsp fresh lemon juice

Shaved orange zest (obtained by using a microplane)

¼ cup vanilla sugar (pg. 150)

2 Tbsp Grand Marnier liqueur

Dusting of nutmeg

1 almond nut pie shell, prebaked (pg. 165)

3 Tbsp all-purpose white flour

1 oz unsalted butter

Juice of drained apples plus Apple Glace (pg. 29) to make 1 cup

1 tsp plain gelatin

Fresh whipped cream (pg. 149)

Dusting of cinnamon and powdered sugar

¼ cup almond pralines (see next page)

Procedure

Core, peel, and slice the apples. Marinate sliced apples overnight in lemon juice, the shaved orange zest, vanilla sugar, Grand Marnier, and nutmeg. The following day drain apples of all liquid. Reserve the liquid. Prepare the almond nut shell. Coat the drained apples well with flour, being sure no lumps of flour remain. Place the apple slices into the crust and dot the apples with the butter. Bake in a preheated oven at 375 degrees for 45 minutes.

Combine the juice of the drained apples with apple glace to make 1 cup. Over a low flame bring it just to a simmering point and gently dissolve gelatin in it. Evenly pour the mixture over the baked pie. Refrigerate the pie until completely cooled. Bring pie back to room temperature. Serve it decorated with swirls of fresh whipped cream, a dusting of cinnamon and powdered sugar, and the almond pralines.

Almond Pralines

YIELD: 6 cups

Ingredients

1 lb raw almonds, lightly toasted and sliced

3 cups superfine sugar

¼ cup lemon extract

2 Tbsp lemon zest

Preparation

Toast the almonds in a preheated oven at 400 degrees to a light hue. In a saucepan, melt the sugar to a light brown color. As soon as sugar is ready, add the nuts and coat them well with the caramel. Very carefully stir in the lemon extract and lemon zest. Line a sheet pan with lightly oiled parchment paper, spread the nut mixture evenly out over the paper and set it in a cool place until completely hardened. Break mixture into small pieces and grind in a food processor to a medium coarse consistency. Store in an airtight container in a cool, dark place. Refrigerate after opening.

Macadamia Chocolate Truffle Tart

YIELD: 1 9-inch tart

Ingredients

1 9-inch pre-baked tart shell (pg. 166)

4 oz dark semisweet chocolate

½ cup heavy cream

½ cup vanilla sugar (pg. 150)

¼ cup dark flavorful rum

5 oz mascarpone, softened to room temperature

~12 oz fresh raspberries

2 cups Apple Glace (pg. 29)

Fresh whipped cream for garnish (pg. 149)

2 Tbsp shaved dark chocolate

Procedure

Prepare the tart shell. Melt the chocolate over a double boiler. Set aside to lightly cool it. Whip heavy cream with vanilla sugar until soft peaks form. Slowly incorporate the rum and gently fold cream into softened mascarpone. Do not over-mix. Very carefully incorporate the cooled chocolate. *Caution:* Mascarpone easily separates if over-mixed. Fill tart shell with mixture. Garnish with fresh raspberries and lightly glace with apple glace. Refrigerate tart for about 1 hour or until glace is set and firm. Decorate with dollops of freshly whipped cream and sprinkle the shaved chocolate over it. To serve, place tart in a pool of apple glace.

Macadamia Raspberry Tart

YIELD: 1 9-inch tart; 10 servings

Ingredients

1 9-inch pre-baked tart shell
(pg. 165)

Pastry Cream (pg. 149)

1 dry pint fresh raspberries

½ cup Apple Glace (pg. 29)

Fresh whipped cream (pg. 149)

Procedure

Prepare the tart shell using macadamia nuts, and let cool. Spread pastry cream evenly on tart shell. Arrange raspberries in tight circles, starting on the outside rim and working towards the center. Spoon cooled apple glace over raspberries, being sure that the glace is not hot, as it would ruin the pastry cream. Decorate the tart with fresh whipped cream.

Bourbon Chocolate Pecan Pie

YIELD: 1 9-inch pie (10–12 servings)

Ingredients

1 unbaked pie shell (pg. 166)

3 oz dark semisweet chocolate,
shaved

3 oz white chocolate, shaved

1 large whole egg

2 large egg yolks

3 oz vanilla sugar (pg. 150)

4 oz mascarpone,
at room temperature

2 oz Tennessee sour mash whiskey

1 oz lemon extract

4 oz toasted pecans, finely ground

Fresh whipped cream for garnish
(pg. 149)

Toasted pecan halves for garnish

Powdered sugar for garnish

Procedure

Prepare pie shell. Place both shaved chocolates over double boiler and slowly melt. Turn off heat as soon as melted. In mixing bowl, combine eggs, egg yolks, and sugar, and beat on high speed until they are fluffy and somewhat lemon colored. Slowly add the mascarpone and combine well. Incorporate the sour mash whiskey and lemon extract. Remove bowl from mixer and fold in pecans. With a plastic spatula, swiftly whisk in melted warm chocolate. Fill unbaked pie shell with mixture and bake in preheated oven at 375 degrees for 45 minutes. Rotate the pie and bake for another 20 minutes. Remove from oven and place on cooling rack. Divide the pie while still warm with a sharp slicing knife dipped in hot water for each slice. Garnish with rosettes of fresh whipped cream and toasted pecan halves, and lightly dust with powdered sugar.

CUSTARDS AND ICE CREAMS

Crème Brûlée
YIELD: 4 servings

Needed
4   4-oz ramekins

Ingredients
1 cup heavy cream

2 Tbsp vanilla sugar (pg. 150)

10 large egg yolks

1 tsp apricot liqueur

1 tsp lemon extract

1 tsp brown sugar

Edible flowers and mint leaves for garnish

Procedure
In a saucepan, bring cream to scalding point. Do not boil. In a bowl, combine vanilla sugar with egg yolks, and beat at high speed until thick. Reduce speed and slowly incorporate apricot liqueur, lemon extract, and scalded cream. Transfer to a stainless steel bowl. Set it over a simmering water bath, being careful to keep the water from touching the bottom of the bowl, and whisk continuously until well thickened. The cream should reach 155 degrees. Transfer the custard into the 4 ramekins and refrigerate for 4 hours. The custard needs to be completely cold. Sprinkle the brown sugar over the custard and, with a blowtorch, carefully and quickly caramelize the sugar, being careful not to heat the custard. Garnish with edible flowers and mint leaves.

Crème Caramel

YIELD: 4 servings

Needed

    4 5-oz ramekins

Ingredients

Poaching pan, big enough to hold 4 ramekins

Cotton cloth

Cooking spray

½ cup caramel

1 cup whole milk

Inside pulp of a ¼ vanilla bean or seedpods

1 cup heavy cream

4 whole eggs

¾ cup vanilla sugar (pg. 150)

1 Tbsp apricot liqueur

1 Tbsp lemon extract

Fresh whipped cream for garnish (pg. 149)

Edible flowers and mint leaves for garnish

Procedure

Line the poaching pan with the cotton cloth. Spray sides and bottoms of the ramekins with the cooking spray, and place them on the cloth in the pan. Place equal amounts of caramel into ramekins. In a saucepan, combine the milk and vanilla pulp. Add the cream and bring to scalding point—do not boil. Keep it warm. In a bowl, combine eggs with vanilla sugar and mix at high speed until well thickened. Add liqueur and lemon extract and combine it well. Reduce speed and slowly add the scalded milk-cream. Mix it until well combined.

Ladle the custard into prepared ramekins. If the mixture is quite foamy, wait 15–20 minutes for the froth to subside, then continue to fill the cups. Fill the poaching pan ⅓ full with hot water. Cover very tightly with aluminum foil and place in preheated oven at 425 degrees and poach for 45 minutes. Test for doneness of the custard by gently inserting a clean knife. If the knife comes out clean, the cream is done. If not, continue poaching for another 10–15 minutes. Care must be taken, though, not to overcook them. This could result in a scrambled, gritty consistency rather than smooth and creamy. Remove the ramekins as fast as possible from the hot water and place them on a cooling rack. Refrigerate at least 3 hours before unmolding them.

Serving Procedure

With a sharp pointed knife, loosen the custard from the sides of the cup. Place upside down on a serving plate and gently shake the custard loose. Scrape out remaining caramel. Decorate with rosettes of fresh whipped cream, violets or other edible flowers, and mint leaves.

Chocolate Mousse

YIELD: 4 servings

Ingredients

4 oz dark semisweet chocolate, shaved

4 oz white chocolate, shaved

4 large egg yolks

2 Tbsp vanilla sugar (pg. 150), divided

½ cup heavy cream

1 tsp white crème de menthe

2 large egg whites

Fresh whipped cream for garnish (pg. 149)

Toasted almonds for garnish

Lady fingers for garnish

Procedure

To shave the chocolate, hold a wrapped square of chocolate in the hand to warm it slightly. Unwrap and shave chocolate using a vegetable peeler or small sharp knife. Place the dark chocolate in bottom of a stainless steel bowl. Place the white on top and melt it over a simmering water bath, not touching the water, stirring it occasionally with a wooden spoon. Do not use aluminum utensils for this. As soon as chocolate is melted, remove it from the water bath.

Place egg yolks with 1 Tbsp of sugar in mixing bowl and mix at high speed until thick and creamy. Incorporate well with the cooled chocolate. In a separate bowl, add half of the remaining sugar to the cream and whip it until stiff peaks form. Incorporate the crème de menthe. Carefully fold, do not mix, the cream into the chocolate-egg mixture. In a bowl, whip the egg whites to stiff peaks. Add the rest of the sugar to it. Mix it well and carefully stir the egg whites into the mousse. The mousse needs to stay fluffy and airy, so do not over-mix.

Refrigerate the mousse for at least 3 hours. Flavor will improve with aging. If properly refrigerated, the mousse will keep up to 5 days and greatly improve in flavor. Decorate the mousse with fresh whipped cream, toasted almonds, and lady fingers.

**FAWN BROOK
FAMILY MEMORIES**

Chocolate Mousse

After a hard day at play came the reward at the end of the evening when my dad would clean out the kitchen pantry and refrigerators. We would anxiously await the much coveted chocolate mousse vat. This dreamy, heaven sent, stainless steel bowl held the most amazing melt-in-your-mouth confection on the face of the earth. I have tried for years to duplicate the intoxicating dessert, tried countless varieties at restaurants everywhere, and never have I been able to match the taste of my dad's chocolate mousse. The clouds of egg whites mixed with the creamy smooth chocolate become a combination of unbelievable satisfaction.

Iced Grand Marnier Orange Soufflé

YIELD: 4 servings

Ingredients

4 large thick-skinned oranges

2 oz vanilla sugar, plus 1 Tbsp (pg. 150)

8 large egg yolks

½ oz rose petal syrup (pg. 29)

½ oz lemon extract

1 oz Grand Marnier liqueur

½ cup crème fraîche (pg. 25)

1 Tbsp fine shavings of orange zest

½ cup heavy cream

3 large egg whites

Hot syrup (see below)

Fresh whipped cream (pg. 149)

Dusting of powdered sugar

Edible flowers or candied flowers for garnish

Procedure

Cut off tops of oranges, about ¼-inch thick. Cut off a sliver on the bottom, just enough to keep orange from rolling. With a flexible serrated small fruit knife, loosen the pulp and with a fruit spoon twist out the pulp, being sure *not* to damage the shell. Scrape out all the pulp and set aside. Place the shells upside down on a tray. Wrap with plastic and freeze until shells are hard, about 8 hours.

To make the custard filling, add 2 oz of the sugar to egg yolks and beat at high speed until the eggs are very thick. Incorporate the rose syrup, lemon extract, Grand Marnier liqueur, and crème fraîche. In a separate bowl, whip the heavy cream until stiff peaks form. Fold this into the egg yolks. Whip the egg whites until they start to form peaks. Incorporate the rest of the sugar and whip until soft peaks form. Fold it into the egg mixture. Do not over-mix it, as the cream needs to stay airy and fluffy. Chill thoroughly.

Fill the frozen orange shells with half of the chilled but not frozen custard. Freeze them until well set. Finish filling them with the rest of the custard. Freeze them until hard on top, 9–10 hours. You may double wrap them with plastic wrap and freeze for later use.

Squeeze out all juice from pulp, reserving 1 cup for the hot syrup. Drain the hot syrup over the orange tops. Refrigerate the tops until ready to use.

Serving Suggestion

Place a swirl of fresh whipped cream on a plate and set orange on it to keep it in place. Set the top aside. Create a swirl of whipped cream on top of the orange. Place the top in a slanted position on the side of the whipped cream and generously dust top with powdered sugar. Decorate with a mint leaf and an edible small flower, such as a violet or Johnny Jump-Up, or a candied flower and angelica, etc.

Hot Syrup
Ingredients

1 cup juice reserved from the oranges	Small cinnamon stick
½ cup vanilla sugar	3 whole cloves
1 star anise	

Procedure

In a saucepan add orange juice, ½ cup vanilla sugar, 1 star anise, a small cinnamon stick, and a few whole cloves. Stir until all sugar is dissolved. Bring to a boil. Reduce heat and gently simmer until a light syrupy consistency is achieved.

White Chocolate Strawberry Parfait

YIELD: 6 servings

Needed

Pâté pan with hinged sides, 8 x 4 inches and 3 inches deep; parchment paper to line bottom and sides of pan

Ingredients

1st layer:

   2 cups firmly packed sliced fresh strawberries

   ¼ cup fresh squeezed lemon juice

   ¼ cup fine granulated sugar

   10 large egg yolks

   ½ cup heavy cream

   1 oz unsalted butter

   ¼ cup strawberry liqueur

   1 drop of red food coloring

   3 oz fine shaved white chocolate

2nd Layer:

   1 oz fine sugar

   1 cup heavy cream

Garnish:

   2 medium-sized fresh strawberries, halved

   Sliced angelica strips, inserted into halved strawberries

   Strawberry fan

   Sprig of fresh mint

   Fresh whipped cream (pg. 149)

Procedure

Cover sliced strawberries with lemon juice. Combine sugar and egg yolks and whip at high speed until nicely thickened. In a saucepan, add butter to ½ cup of cream and bring to scalding point—do not boil. To thickened eggs, add liqueur and food coloring. Add strawberries and lemon juice, and incorporate well. Slowly add scalded cream and again mix well. Place mixture in stainless-steel bowl and set over double boiler, being sure water level does not touch the bowl. Never let the water boil over, rather a constant simmering point must be kept. Continuously whip the mixture until well thickened. Remove from water bath, and with a plastic spatula, fold in shaved white chocolate.

Line pan—bottom and sides—with parchment paper, being sure there is enough paper to overlap the top of the parfait since the parfait has to be frozen and the overlapping paper will prevent freezer burn. Place the parfait carefully in prepared pan, but only half full. Gently shake the pan and carefully pull the paper to prevent air pockets, and also to fill the sides and corners evenly with the mixture. Place parfait without covering in freezer for about 3 hours or until well set and firm, but not frozen. Place remaining parfait mixture in cooler.

(continued)

Add 1 oz of sugar to 1 cup of whipping cream and whip until stiff peaks form. Gently fold the cream into leftover parfait mixture. Remove parfait pan from freezer. Cut strawberries in half, insert a generous sliver of angelica and place the berries cut side down on parfait. Fill the pan with the remaining parfait mixture. Gently and carefully pull parchment paper over parfait. Double wrap the whole pan with plastic wrap and place in freezer for 24 hours. Remove all paper from parfait and slice it carefully into equal portions with a sharp hot wet knife. Garnish with a strawberry fan, a sprig of mint, and a dollop of fresh whipped cream.

Vanilla Ice Cream

YIELD: 1½ quarts

Ingredients

1 vanilla bean
1½ cups super fine sugar, divided
15 large egg yolks
1½ Tbsp rose petal syrup (pg. 29)
1½ Tbsp lemon extract
¼ cup instant vanilla powder
¼ cup crème fraîche (pg. 25)
1 cup heavy cream
3 large egg whites

Procedure

A day ahead of time, split vanilla bean in half lengthwise. With a small spoon, scrape out the seedpod and combine it with the sugar. Seal the container airtight. Use the rest of the bean for vanilla sugar. In a bowl, add 1 cup of the sugar to egg yolks and beat at high speed until the eggs are very thick. Incorporate the rose syrup, lemon extract, vanilla powder, and crème fraîche. In a separate bowl, add ¼ cup of the sugar to cream and whip until stiff peaks form. Fold this into the egg yolks. In a bowl, whip the egg whites until they start to form peaks. Incorporate the rest of the sugar and whip until soft peaks form. Fold it into the egg mixture. Do not over-mix it, as the cream needs to stay airy and fluffy. Cover and freeze for 24 hours before use.

Lemon Apricot Ice Cream

Add 1 oz of apricot liqueur, plus very fine zest of ½ a lemon, to the egg yolks in the above recipe. Proceed as outlined for Vanilla Ice Cream.

Raspberry Bavarian Cream

YIELD: 6 Servings

Ingredients

1 cup heavy cream

2 Tbsp vanilla sugar (pg. 150)

10 large egg yolks

1 tsp apricot liqueur

1 tsp lemon extract

6 oz fresh raspberries, or berries of choice

Fresh whipped cream for garnish (pg. 149)

4 mint leaves for garnish

Berries or small edible flowers for garnish

Procedure

In a saucepan, bring cream to a scalding point, but do not boil. In mixing bowl, combine vanilla sugar with egg yolks and beat at high speed until thick. Reduce speed and slowly incorporate apricot liqueur, lemon extract, and scalded cream. Combine well and transfer to a stainless-steel bowl, set it over a simmering water bath (bowl not touching water) and whisk continuously until well thickened. The cream should reach 155 degrees.

Evenly distribute the berries into six 6-oz champagne bowls, ladle the custard over the berries, and refrigerate until cold. Garnish each with a dollop of fresh whipped cream, a mint leaf, and berries or small edible flowers.

Adrieke and Chris, 1993

COOKIES

Scandinavian Ginger Cookies
(can also be used for Gingerbread Men)
YIELD: 68–70 cookies, or 23 gingerbread men

Ingredients
6 oz unsalted butter

¾ cup brown sugar, firmly packed

1 Tbsp ground cinnamon

1½ tsp ground cloves

2 Tbsp ground ginger

¼ cup boiling water

1 tsp baking soda

2½ cups all purpose white flour

Procedure
Whip the butter until fluffy. In a separate bowl, combine sugar, cinnamon, cloves, and ginger. Add to the butter and mix well. Stir baking soda into boiling water and add it to the mixture. Mix in flour and beat until a stiff elastic dough is achieved. If necessary, add a few more drops of hot water. Form a ball, wrap it in plastic wrap and chill for 30 minutes. Divide dough in half, and on a well-floured board roll dough out to about ⅛-inch thick. Cut out the cookies with a 2½ x 1½-inch cookie cutter. Place them on a coated sheet pan. Bake in preheated oven at 375 degrees for 15 minutes. Reverse pan and bake for another 15 minutes. Remove from oven and place cookies on a cooling rack. Store in an airtight container.

Icing for Gingerbread Men
Ingredients
1 cup powdered sugar

1½ tsp cold water

Procedure
Mix water and sugar to a nice consistency. Decorate the men as quickly as possible, as icing will dry in no time.

Almond Rum Cookies

YIELD: about 30 cookies

Ingredients

14 oz sifted all-purpose white flour, plus extra to roll out the dough

4 oz blanched almonds, ground

½ tsp salt

1 lb unsalted butter

1 cup powered sugar, firmly packed

4 Tbsp light rum

1 tsp cinnamon oil extract

Powdered sugar for dusting

Procedure

Whisk together the flour, almonds, and salt. In a mixing bowl, cream the butter with the sugar until light and fluffy. Beat in the rum and cinnamon extract; blend it well. Reduce the speed and slowly incorporate the flour mixture. Place the dough in a container, cover with plastic wrap and refrigerate for about 4 hours until dough is firm and cold.

Because the dough gets sticky, cut it into three sections, and work with one section at a time while the others remain refrigerated. Working with a small amount of dough, knead it until pliable. Roll it out on a well-floured tabletop to about ⅓-inch thickness. Cut out cookies with a 2½-inch scalloped cookie cutter and transfer the cookies with a metal spatula to a well-oiled cookie sheet. With a decorative ½-inch cookie cutter, cut out the center of half of the cookies. They will serve as the top of the cookie sandwich. Bake cookies in a preheated oven at 350 degrees for about 20–25 minutes or until the cookies take on a light golden hue.

Rum Cream Filling
Ingredients

3 oz unsalted softened butter

8 oz powdered sugar

½ oz light rum

2½ Tbsp heavy cream

Procedure

Whip the butter with the sugar until creamy. Slowly incorporate the rum and heavy cream. Whip until well combined. Cover with plastic wrap and place in a cool place until ready to use. *Do not refrigerate.* Place a small amount of the filling in the center of a solid cookie. Gently top it with a cut out one and generously dust cookies with powdered sugar. Refrigerate until ready to use. A word of caution: cookies are very brittle, so handle with care. Also be sure that the work surface is cool rather than warm.

Marmalade-filled Almond Rum Cookies

YIELD: about 30 cookies

Ingredients

1 lb softened cool butter

4 large egg yolks

1 cup vanilla sugar (pg. 150)

Fine zest of 1 medium lemon

4 cups blanched almonds, finely ground

2 Tbsp rose petal syrup (pg. 29)

¼ cup dark rum

4 cups all-purpose white flour

Various marmalades—apricot, raspberry, etc.

Extra vanilla sugar and powdered sugar for dusting

Chocolate Glace (pg. 159)

Procedure

Combine butter, egg yolks, vanilla sugar, and lemon zest in mixing bowl and whip until mixture gets creamy. Slowly incorporate ground almonds. Add syrup and rum and slowly add the flour. Incorporate well. Finish off dough with your hands. Add more ground almonds if needed. Wrap in plastic wrap and keep in cool place. Line a baking pan with parchment paper. On a lightly floured board roll dough out to ⅛-inch thickness. With a round cutter, cut out the cookies and place on a baking sheet. Bake at 325 degrees in preheated oven for 25 minutes.

Fix another baking pan and cut out equal amounts of cookies, removing the center part of the dough, and again bake them as the previous cookies. Spread the solid cookies with various marmalades and lightly dust with vanilla sugar. Place cookie rings on marmalade cookies. Dust with powdered sugar and bake for another 15 minutes. Bake the center cut-outs and lightly coat with melted chocolate glace. Incorporate on top of the round cookies.

Almond Biscotti

YIELD: 4 12-inch loafs

Ingredients

4 cups all-purpose white flour

¼ tsp salt

2 tsp baking soda

6 large eggs

2 cups vanilla sugar (pg. 150)

1 tsp almond extract

½ cup toasted almonds

Procedure

Preheat the oven to 400 degrees. Line two half-sheet pans with double parchment. Sift together the flour, salt, and baking soda and set aside. Combine the eggs, sugar, and almond extract with the paddle attachment of the mixer until well combined. Fold in the dry ingredients (except almonds) combining well. Fold in the almonds. On a well-floured surface, turn out the batter. Divide the batter into four equal parts. Flour the half-sheet pans well, and place two of the portions on each. Using as much flour as needed, shape the batter into skinny logs. Bake for about 20 minutes, or until pretty firm to the touch.

Let cool for at least 15 minutes and cut into ¼-inch slices, and bake again at 200 degrees for 1 hour, or until very dry and crisp.

**FAWN BROOK
FAMILY MEMORIES**

It's more than a building, more than a restaurant, more than a home. It's the love of our family surrounding us and holding us close. That's what the Fawn Brook and my mom and dad mean to me. It is a place dear to my heart, a haven of love and strength, a blanket of safety and security. My mom and dad have created a home for more than just their family, but for hundreds of individuals, some with names and faces that come year after year and others who visit once, but who retain the memory of a very special night, at a small rustic cabin, in a tiny town nestled high in the Colorado mountains.

Vanilla Almond Crescents

YIELD: 50 crescents

Ingredients

½ cup vanilla sugar (pg. 150)

2½ cups all-purpose white flour

½ cup blanched almonds, finely ground

8 oz butter

1 Tbsp fine lemon zest

2 large egg yolks

2 tsp lemon extract

Vanilla sugar and powdered sugar for dusting

Procedure

It is important to keep the butter and eggs cold and to work in a cool place. Combine sugar, flour, blanched almonds, and zest in a large enough mixing bowl. Cube the butter into small cubes and mix with dry ingredients (a dough hook works best), until a gritty consistency is achieved. Add the egg yolks one at a time, and the lemon extract, and mix at a gentle speed until a ball forms. Finish dough off by rolling it in your hands. Wrap it in plastic wrap and keep it in a cool place.

Line a baking pan with parchment paper. Divide dough into small balls, about ½ ounce each. Roll them out by hand, preferably on a cool marble slab, to about 3 inches long. Form them into even-sized crescents. Place them ½-inch apart on baking pan. Bake in preheated oven at 325 degrees for 20 minutes. Remove from oven and generously dust them with vanilla sugar. Return to oven and bake for another 10 minutes. Again, remove them from the oven and generously dust them with powdered sugar. Cool them and then store in an airtight container. Flavor will improve with aging.

Adrieke, Chris, and boys, 2008.

Marzipan

Almond Paste

YIELD: 2½ lbs

Ingredients

12 oz sliced raw almonds

3 cups super fine sugar

3 egg whites

Procedure

Grind the almonds to a fine consistency and combine with the sugar. In a separate bowl, lightly beat the eggs to a foaming stage. Place the sugar mixture in a mixing bowl and with a dough hook mix it while slowly adding the beaten egg whites. Slowly mix it until a smooth elastic paste is achieved. If the paste is too sticky, add a little more sugar to it, a teaspoon at a time. Double wrap the almond paste in plastic wrap and refrigerate until ready to use. Almond paste can be kept in freezer for 8–10 months and under proper refrigeration up to 5 months. Bring to room temperature before using.

Marzipan

YIELD: 4½ lbs

Ingredients

4 large egg whites

3 Tbsp Amaretto liqueur

1 Tbsp lemon extract

2½ lb almond paste (see above)

6 cups super fine sugar, divided

Procedure

Slightly beat the egg whites, then whisk together the egg whites, Amaretto, and lemon extract. Place almond paste in separate mixing bowl, add 2 cups of the sugar and mix well. Slowly add the egg mixture. Keep mixing and add the remaining sugar, small amounts at a time, and combine well. Double wrap the finished product in plastic wrap and refrigerate until needed. Bring to room temperature before using. As with almond paste, marzipan can be kept in the same way. Flavor will greatly improve with aging.

Marzipan Roll

YIELD: 1 roll, approximately 6 servings

Ingredients

8 oz marzipan (pg. 184)

1 large egg yolk

Fine zest of 1 small lemon

6 oz puff pastry (pg. 64)

Egg wash (pg. 3)

Vanilla Sauce (pg. 148)

Procedure

Incorporate lemon zest and egg yolk with marzipan. On a floured surface, preferably a cool marble slab, roll out the puff pastry to a rectangle about 9 x 10 inches. Form marzipan into an 8-inch long rope. Lightly wet puff pastry with cold water. Place marzipan rope on pastry and tightly roll it up, being sure that the seam of the pastry is to the bottom. Seal off the ends and carefully bend the roll into a horseshoe shape. Decorate with pastry stars, brush with egg wash and place it in the freezer for 12 hours. Egg wash the roll again and bake it in a preheated oven at 500 degrees for about 15 minutes or until golden brown. Serve warm with vanilla sauce.

**FAWN BROOK
FAMILY MEMORIES**

Weddings

Over the past three decades, the pine log and moss rock structure of the Fawn Brook Inn, with its warm, welcoming rooms and fairy tale garden, has been the setting of choice for countless wedding engagements, weddings, receptions, and anniversaries. From simple proposals where a nervous groom-to-be could hardly afford a ring, to lavish affairs with Hollywood celebrities, Hermann and Mieke have played host to them all. Still, not even a wedding whose guests included Robert Redford, could hold a match to the scene in the fall of 2005, when Kara and Kajetan were married. It was not only appropriate, but absolutely perfect, for the entire mountain community of Allenspark, who had done so much to raise Kajetan, to be in attendance.

Truffles

Chestnut Caramel Truffles

YIELD: about 80 truffles

Ingredients

1½ lb chestnuts

3 cups super fine sugar

¼ cup lemon extract

16 oz shaved white chocolate (pg. 00)

12 oz softened unsalted butter

2 lbs marzipan (pg. 00)

2 Tbsp lemon zest

¼ oz dark well-flavored rum

Preparation

Carefully toast chestnuts in a 475-degree oven until dry (remaining weight about 1 lb). Line a sheet pan with lightly oiled parchment paper. Chop the toasted chestnuts into small pieces. In a heavy saucepan, melt the sugar to a light caramel color. Carefully incorporate lemon extract and evenly spread the caramel over oiled parchment paper. Place in a cool place to harden. Melt the chocolate over a hot, but *not* boiling, water bath. Remove from heat source and cool it down. In mixing bowl, beat the butter until creamy. Slowly incorporate chestnuts, marzipan, lemon zest, and rum. Carefully fold in cooled-down chocolate and refrigerate until firm.

Break caramel into small pieces and grind in food processor to a medium coarse praline consistency. Form small balls from the cooled down marzipan/chestnut and chocolate mixture, about 1 ounce each, and refrigerate to harden. Roll them through the caramel praline and refrigerate until set. Roll them through a second time until well coated. Refrigerate until set again, then wrap them individually in foil or place in truffle cups.

Almond Chocolate Truffles

YIELD: about 80 truffles

Ingredients

1 lb raw slivered almonds

3 cups superfine sugar

¼ cup lemon extract

1 lb shaved dark semi-sweet chocolate

12 oz unsalted butter, softened

2 Tbsp lemon zest

¼ cup dark well-flavored rum

3 cups shaved dark chocolate to coat finished truffles

Preparation

Toast the almonds in a pre-heated oven at 400 degrees to a light hue. In heavy saucepan, melt the sugar to a light brown color. As soon as sugar is ready add the nuts and mix well, being sure almonds are well coated with caramel. Very carefully stir in the lemon extract. Line a sheet pan with lightly oiled parchment paper. Spread nut mixture out evenly over oiled paper and set in a cool place until completely hardened. Break hardened mixture into small pieces and grind in a food processor to a medium coarse consistency.

Slowly melt chocolate over a hot, but *not* boiling, water bath. As soon as the chocolate is melted remove from heat source and let it cool down. In mixing bowl, beat softened butter until creamy and slowly incorporate almond praline. Add the lemon zest and incorporate the rum. Carefully fold in cooled melted chocolate. Refrigerate until set to a firm consistency. Form small balls, about 1 ounce each, and coat them with dark chocolate shavings. Dust them generously with powdered sugar. Refrigerate until firm, then wrap them individually in foil or place in truffle cups.

Macadamia Chocolate Truffles

Proceed as for almond truffles above. Substitute white chocolate for dark, and finish the truffles by rolling them through dark chocolate sprinkles.

Hazelnut White Chocolate Truffles

Proceed as for almond truffles above. Substitute white chocolate for dark, and coat with dark melted chocolate and freshly grated coconut.

Gingerbread House

YIELD: 1 house, 7" long, 8" wide front and back, 7" high to roof line, 10" to center of roof. Balcony level 5" high. Roof line 8" each side, 11"deep. Roof overhang 3" on each side, front overhangs 1½".

STEP 1

Build the frame out of heavy cardboard. Cut out all windows, doors, balcony, etc. Place the frame on a solid foundation, such as a strong plastic or wood board, for once the house is completely built it would be most difficult to move it again.

Solid Ingredients for the House

Icing Glue
Ingredients

1 cup superfine sugar

1 extra large white egg

¼ Tbsp cream of tartar

¼ cup boiling water

Procedure

Combine all ingredients and whisk until stiff peaks form. Use right away.

Italian Meringue
Ingredients

1 lb superfine sugar

3½ oz water

7 extra large egg whites

Procedure

Combine 12 oz of sugar with the water and heat it to 245 degrees. In a bowl, add the remaining sugar to the egg whites and beat until stiff peaks form. Very slowly incorporate the cooled sugar-water mixture and again beat it until stiff peaks form.

Gelatin
Ingredients

8 oz boiling water

1½ oz plain gelatin

Procedure

Bring water to a fast boil, turn off heat and quickly whisk in gelatin until completely dissolved. Keep it warm over a candle light.

Almond Hazelnut Dough for House Frame
Ingredients

    1 cup vanilla sugar (pg. 150)

    5 whole extra large eggs

    8 oz all-purpose white flour

    16 oz toasted ground almonds

    16 oz toasted ground hazelnuts

    1 tsp each freshly ground cloves, allspice, cinnamon, nutmeg

    4 oz candied ginger, finely chopped

    Dusting of salt

    1 Tbsp each lemon and orange zest

Procedure

Have all ingredients ready. Combine vanilla sugar with eggs and whip until they are creamy and lemon-colored. Slowly add the flour and combine well. Slowly add half of the ground almonds and all of the hazelnuts. Add the spices and again incorporate well. Add the ginger and salt, remove the dough from the bowl, and divide in four equal portions. On a clean flat surface spread out the reserved ground almonds and roll individual dough in it until almonds are well incorporated. Place dough in plastic wrap and refrigerate overnight. *Dough will improve greatly with age. It can be refrigerated up to four months.*

Assembling the Frame of the House

Line inside of windows with a clear or transparent paper and glue them into the inside openings. Glue all house sections together with a non-toxic glue. Do not attach the roof panels yet. Let the house dry for at least 24 hours.

STEP 2

Line sheet pans with parchment paper. On a cool surface, preferably a marble slab, roll out individual sections of the dough about ¼-inch thick. Measure all sections according to the house dimensions, keeping them a little larger, as the dough will shrink during baking procedure. Bake the sections in a preheated oven at 375 degrees for 30 minutes. Remove from oven and quickly cut out all windows, doors, etc., while dough is still warm. Reserve cut-outs for decoration purposes. Trim the edge of each section to the exact measurements. Cool all sections completely before assembling the house.

STEP 3

Prepare and bake Scandinavian ginger cookies (pg. 179), 76 cookies for the roof shingles and 2 stars. Also bake gingerbread men (same cookie recipe) for decoration purposess.

STEP 4

Very lightly coat house sections with icing glue, one section at a time. Attach them to cardboard frame, holding them firmly in place until glue is set and dry. If needed, use T-pins—carefully, though, since the dry dough cracks easily. Attach cardboard roof to the house and let it dry for 3 hours.

STEP 5

Out of 16½ oz of marzipan (pg. 184), form the following:

   2 oz for chimney

   4 oz for two 5¼-inch-long round columns

   1½ oz for an 8-inch-long balcony

   6 oz for four fence posts, each post having two 4-inch-long crossbars

   3 oz for two 5-inch-long fence railings on side of house

Procedure

Form all these items, and let them dry before using.

STEP 6

Lightly brush underside of the ginger cookies with icing glue and attach them to the roof, starting at the bottom edge and letting them overhang about ⅛-inch. Start at the left side with the first row, going to the right; place second row overlapping the first row by ½ inch. The effect should be that of a tiled roof. Attach the chimney with the icing glue before finishing the last row.

Basic Decorating Materials

Italian meringue, clear warm gelatin, stick pins, clear assorted glass beads, marzipan, gingerbread men, pine nuts, star anise, pistachios, candied angelica, licorice sticks, gum drops in different colors, sliced almonds, artificial birds, trees, and all different kinds of embellishments.

Last Steps of Finishing the House

With icing glue and pins if needed, attach the columns for the balcony on each side of the house; attach the balcony, and secure with T-pins. Attach window sills and doors, leaving door halfway ajar. For the balcony railing, pipe out Italian meringue along the outside, and let it harden. Place two pine nuts lengthwise with a small red bead on the top on stick pins, and insert them in the hardened meringue so a railing is formed. Place a small amount of Italian meringue in a pastry bag fitted with a small decorative nozzle and decorate door panels and windows.

To fasten any decorative items, place dollops of meringue in desired places and press star anise, pistachios, almonds, etc., in flower designs. Stick any decorative material on a needle, place in warm clear gelatin, and attach it at desired position, holding it just for a few seconds until secured. Keep gelatin warm over a low candle flame.

Place clear assorted glass beads on string and form icicles in various lengths, placing them along the roofline. Fasten them with stick pins, and decorate entire roofline with dollops of meringue. Decorate the chimney with meringue and red licorice; decorate windows with angelica and birds; build a fence around the house. Decorate with small pine cones, etc. Place small artificial trees and shrubs around the house; place small birds and animals around it, and generously dust the entire roof with powdered sugar.

Place a small light inside the house. Make a walkway with trail mix. Place small meringue dollops along the walkway and place pretzels in them to create a fence line. Place gingerbread men in front of the house holding candy canes, and just let your imagination flow to finish surrounding area.

FAWN BROOK
FAMILY MEMORIES

The Gingerbread House

My father is an amazing man with a mind for endless creativity, demanding of perfection, and hair-brained, irrational ideas. One Christmas he decided it would be fun to make a gingerbread house to display in the restaurant. Sounds simple enough, many a shoe box gingerbread houses grace holiday decorations. But . . . this is Hermann. A simple little gingerbread house is NOT acceptable to create. Oh no, this house became a Swiss chalet large enough to become a mansion for Santa's elves. I went down to help my dad assemble this house one evening, thinking it would be a fun time to "bond" with my dear old dad. Bond we did . . . to the house, the icicles, the fence, the roof, the windows, doors, and each detail that was glued on with icing. Not the bonding I had in mind, but for year after year, the house was a treat for the customers and a fond memory for me.

LOOKING BACK,

30 years have passed since we started our journey as a family at the Fawn Brook Inn.

Little did we know what was ahead of us, but a lot did happen during that time, not only within our family but also with so many people who entered through our doors.

Yes, we shared in the joy of so many occasions, but also in times of discouragement and grief.

Those who came as strangers became friends or sometimes even extended families and their lives left a lasting impact in our hearts.

Grateful we are for all those years with so many wonderful people who made the Fawn Brook Inn what it is today, grateful for our staff and all those who helped us, their presence reflecting on who we are.

LOOKING AHEAD,

We don't know which road the rest of our journey will lead us, but this we know that God's Angels will carry the banner of His grace, protection, courage and strength over us wherever we go.

With love and gratitude,

Mieke.

Creating the
Perfect Menu

To plan a correct and pleasing menu is almost like composing a classical masterpiece. Certain steps must be followed to successfully please your audience. There are 14 steps to keep in mind.

I. Do not repeat the same meat, fowl, or fish on the same menu, even if the preparations are different.

II. Ensure a variety of colors on alternated courses. Avoid a white sauce for fish as first course if the main course such as chicken is also to be served with a white sauce.

III. Vary the garnishes from course to course. Avoid using the same vegetables for all courses, even as a separate course.

IV. Avoid cross cooking, such as boiled fish for first course and boiled meat as the main course. Vary the methods of cooking.

V. Consider the times of the year and weather conditions. Serve heavier, heartier fare in the colder months and lighter fare in the hotter months.

VI. Choose fresh produce, according to season, and take advantage of local farmers' markets offerings. Avoid super market specials.

VII. Do *not* offer fruit at the beginning of a meal if you are planning to use it in a dessert at the end of a meal, such as in a fruit tart, etc.

VIII. Do not start a meal with a rich, creamy sauce if the main course has one. Also, avoid rich creamy desserts at the end of a meal.

IX. Variation is the spice of a good meal, as it is in life.

X. Keep in mind that heavier meals should be accompanied with a lighter savory sauce, rather than a cream sauce.

XI. Remember after a heavy meal, a light dessert is appropriate.

XII. Avoid too many cold courses, even in hot weather.

XIII. When writing out menus, make them clear and understandable. Avoid many foreign names.

XIV. Menus should be written correctly, and make them as pleasant to look at as possible.

Remember, a well-written menu gets digestive juices flowing.

INDEX